THERE IS ALWAYS A WAY.

SPEAKER PROXIMIT

LOVESAC STEALTHTECH

you NEVER KNOW UNTIL you ASK.

SH YOURSELF OUT OF THE NEST.

T0284790

LET ME SAVE YOU
25 YEARS

SHAWN D. NELSON

THERE IS ALWAYS A WAY.

LET ME SAVE YOU 25 YEARS

MISTAKES, MIRACLES, AND LESSONS FROM THE LOVESAC STORY

Forbes | Books

Published by Forbes Books, Charleston, South Carolina.
An imprint of Advantage Media Group.

Forbes Books is a registered trademark, and the Forbes Books colophon is a trademark of Forbes Media, LLC.

Printed in the United States of America.

10 9 8 7 6 5 4 3 2 1

ISBN: 979-8-88750-352-3 (Hardcover)
ISBN: 979-8-88750-353-0 (eBook)

Library of Congress Control Number: 2023914705

Book design by Analisa Smith.

This custom publication is intended to provide accurate information and the opinions of the author in regard to the subject matter covered. It is sold with the understanding that the publisher, Forbes Books, is not engaged in rendering legal, financial, or professional services of any kind. If legal advice or other expert assistance is required, the reader is advised to seek the services of a competent professional.

Since 1917, Forbes has remained steadfast in its mission to serve as the defining voice of entrepreneurial capitalism. Forbes Books, launched in 2016 through a partnership with Advantage Media, furthers that aim by helping business and thought leaders bring their stories, passion, and knowledge to the forefront in custom books. Opinions expressed by Forbes Books authors are their own. To be considered for publication, please visit **books.Forbes.com**.

To Mom. I owe you my life.

CONTENTS

LOVE MATTERS

October 1988. I'm thirteen years old, sprawled out sideways on my own seat in the back of a school bus, headphones on, like a shield to the world, connected to my yellow Sports Edition Sony Walkman that I bought with the money I earned from mowing lawns. I'm feeling good. I'm seventh-grade class president and captain of the Academic Team at Evergreen Junior High School in Salt Lake City, Utah. Most of these other kids on the team are total nerds. They are literally a collection of the most misfit, uncool, lonely people in my grade. We are on our way home from another victory in the Granite District Academic Olympiads. We're undefeated. I'm always an anchor player, leading the "presentation team," tasked to deliver a short skit or multimedia project to be judged for big bonus points. Our part follows the trivia portion of the competition that occurs during the first hour, as we prepare our performance on a surprise topic. I'm creative. I've been on stage as a singer, dancer, and musician all my life. I always lead our little group to deliver a show-stopping routine. We always win. I'm thinking, "They're lucky to have me."

As I'm staring out the window doing the coolest-kid-on-the-bus thing, the song "Everybody Has a Dream" comes on. It's Billy Joel at his best, *The Stranger* album playing on a cassette tape handed down to me by my oldest sister, Kristy. The song meanders through its gospel-style verses laid over a B-3 organ. It crescendos with the soulful chorus repeating its title lyrics on loop. I can't help but survey the smiles on the faces of every "nerd" in school as they're chatting, laughing, and teasing each other on the long bus ride home as this soundtrack echoes in my ears.

The chorus, "Everybody has a dream … everybody has a dream … *everybody has a dream*" repeats over and over again as I watch Poppy, with her tight braids and chronic dried flaky skin under chapped nostrils, laughing and playing hand-slap games with Kathy; David, goofing off with his tucked-in checkered shirt, hiked-up pants, and wavy well-combed hair laid over tor-toiseshell glasses; or Marissa, laughing out loud, jostling her straight-cut bangs over chubby cheeks, her slight eyes pressed tighter thanks to her uniquely warm and perpetual smile.

THESE ARE PEOPLE WITH DREAMS NO LESS THAN MINE, AND I NEED TO LOVE AND RESPECT THEM.

At thirteen years old, I am suddenly overcome with emotion. What is happening to me? I feel something welling up inside. I instantly feel naked and ashamed. Like a bucket of ice water to the face, I am somehow made abruptly and acutely aware of my unwitting bias, attitude, and ignorance toward these sweet people. I am the clown. I am the pitiful one. I am the loner in the back of the bus.

In that moment, at the tender age of thirteen, I experience an epiphany: These *people* are no different from me. They likely have mothers and fathers who believe they are the most incredible souls on earth. They will go on to do amazing things—perhaps even more so than the average "cool" kid in our class. They are equally worthy of every opportunity, accolade, or award. These are people with dreams no less than mine, and I need to love and respect them. I need to love and respect *everyone* for that matter, just by virtue of their existence. *They* put up the bulk of the points for the win that *I* get to share in anyway. *I'm* lucky to have *them*.

In that moment, to the whir of the warm tape player spinning softly in my lap, I learned the most valuable lesson I could possibly acquire in this life. It is a lesson that has stuck with me over the years, even as I have struggled to live up to it along the way: LOVE MATTERS. Then I got off the bus.

As a seventh grader, eighth grader, a brainless high school student, and to this present day as an adult, I am sure to have ebbed in and out of sync with my most profound life lessons and realizations. But decades later now, I still believe *that* moment was some kind of a turning point for me, where even at a young age I developed a fundamental respect for people. I developed the capacity to be touched, to be considerate, and to be humbled by life's subtle lessons. While I wouldn't always demonstrate it day to day, the capacity and humility to see people for who they are, as *equals*, as fellow children of God became fundamental to how I have come to define the biggest of all four-letter words: LOVE.

Love, understood this way, would come to help even the most task-oriented and ambitious version of myself to stop and consider the point of view of others, including friends, business partners, employees, or even adversaries. The understanding and empathy pursuant to this would become a surprisingly powerful tool in business and in leadership ... albeit a topic not often spoken of in such worldly circles.

From this pivotal moment, I developed a *conscience*, some ability to really care, and a willingness to stick my neck out for any underdog. Over time I would become more open-minded, more inviting, more vulnerable, more self-aware, and more willing to self-deprecate and sacrifice my own "face" to help save that of others. With more than twenty-five years of reflec-tion, I have come to realize that this bundle of learned attributes has played a major role in whatever success I have achieved, over and above any raw talent or ability I may have been born with. Love, as a foundational principle, helped make me who I am. But it is the biggest word, and I continue to fall short of it, daily.

In that moment, I also *learned* that I have much to *learn*. This life can teach us the most poignant things in the most unlikely and unpredictable ways if we're willing to *listen* and if we're willing to be brutally honest with ourselves. How could I possibly have known that just ten years later I would accidentally set in motion a series of events that would force-feed me every other important lesson along the way? The story of Lovesac, captured in this book.

And isn't it poetic that twenty years after *that* it would allow me to bring just a *bit* of LOVE to the most barren landscape of all, Wall Street, in the form of a billion-dollar market cap brand (Nasdaq: LOVE) with the opportunity to affect millions of lives for decades to come? And that is just one example. Now twenty-five years into this Lovesac business and counting, I recognize that all I have accomplished never needed to take this long or be quite so difficult in the first place, had I only known then what I have come to know now: Love Matters.

INTRODUCTION

This book is for anyone with aspirations to do anything. The following twenty-five chapters compress the twenty-five-year history to date of Lovesac, a company I set in motion when I was eighteen, into a quick read *with* pictures! These are twenty-five little stories, each followed by twenty-five little lessons that I learned along the way. I call them "Shawnisms."

I've tried to be very honest about my feelings and failings as we go. I've included many of the mistakes and miracles that have added up to some kind of success. Over many years, The Lovesac Company would grow into a billion-dollar publicly traded corporation able to employ thousands. You'll see in a very practical way how these principles can apply to anyone, engaged in anything. If you can learn from *my* mistakes, however, then perhaps *your* ambitions, big or small, can be realized in less than the twenty-five-plus years it has taken me to finally learn something and get somewhere with mine.

But I'm still on the journey myself. Still building. Still reaching. Still trying to wake up tomorrow and do a little better at following my own advice today. It's a never-ending pursuit, but the journey *is* the gift. With an open mind, an honest heart, some ambition, time, help, and a little bit of luck—*all* things are possible. I hope you find that to be true, and I hope this little book can be useful to you as you *make* it so.

So with that, let me save you twenty-five years.

THE FIRST

June 1995. I'm sitting on my parents' couch one summer morning, about ten days after graduating high school. I'm watching *The Price Is Right*, eating a bowl of Cap'n Crunch. A thought enters my brain from wherever thoughts like this come from: "It would be funny to make a really big beanbag—like big enough to fill the whole living room floor." I get off the couch and drive down to the JoAnn Fabrics store on 3300 South in Salt Lake City, Utah, not far from my home.

I'm on a mission to find about ten yards of beanbag chair fabric. The clearance table has a remnant of black vinyl and tan vinyl that should be just enough by my estimates. I race home, shove our couches to the side, and roll the vinyl out across the entire living room floor. Using a baseball as my guide I eyeball and draw two figure-eight patterns on the fuzzy backside of the fabric and cut them out with orange-handled scissors from the penholder next to the phone in our kitchen. I jam my mom's sewing machine. My friend's mom finishes the job, installing a zipper for stuffing. Three weeks of chopping up old blankets, packing peanuts, and camping mattresses in the basement using a wooden paper cutter-chopping-thing from the office closet. Stuffing it took way longer than I thought it would, but the Sac is born.

The very first Sac is out and about, riding along in the back of the truck as an accomplice to all our mindless summer night adventures. Camping. Drive-in movies. Fireworks at the park, rock festivals—everybody loves it. Everybody wants one.

"Where'd you get that thing?" "That's huge!" "I've never seen anything like that!" "Make me one!"

To flop into it is immediately shocking—it's not a beanbag at all. There aren't any beanbag beads in it. Instead, it's filled mostly with chopped-up foam that squishes and forms to your every nook and cranny making you feel weightless. It is an eight-foot-in-diameter comfort cloud that involuntarily puts a smile on anyone's face just to behold its ridiculousness—let alone on contact. But it would be three years until someone finally convinces me to go through the trouble to make another one.

"THE VERY FIRST SAC IS OUT AND ABOUT, RIDING ALONG IN THE BACK OF THE TRUCK AS AN ACCOMPLICE TO ALL OUR MINDLESS SUMMER NIGHT ADVENTURES."

JUST DO SOMETHING

Do it now. Don't wait. Do *something* to take whatever wild idea is nagging at you and see if you can't move it forward—even an inch. Take that first step. Immediately, if you can. Why not? It is amazing what can be learned from actually doing *anything* versus just thinking about it or talking about it forever. Don't think too hard. It may take a thousand starts before one of these ideas takes root and turns into something lasting. This giant beanbag was certainly not the first time in my life I acted decisively and impulsively. This was just another one of my hare-brained schemes brought to life. It is shocking where even the silliest ideas can lead. Lovesac is living proof of this. The world is full of people with good ideas. The thing that separates the champions from the rest is *action*—and then sustained action.

GET OFF THE COUCH, AND GO MAKE SOMETHING HAPPEN.

This disposition to *do* things is not a one-time event either, and it need not apply only to business or entrepreneurship. Whatever our "job" is, we can likely do it better just by *acting* on some of the bright ideas we have, instead of brooding or—worse—complaining about the status quo, unwilling to change it.

How can we build a great culture? How can we get ahead in our career? How can we build better relationships with our partners? How can we get good at something totally new? How can we know what to do next with our lives? How can we grow closer to our families or kids?

Simply *do* the things you think of! Develop a bias for action. Don't wait. Err on the side of *trying* the things that come to your mind without putting them off. Pick up and go. Sign up for the class. Take the risk. Prototype it. Don't just talk—*do*.

Get off the couch (says the couch guy), and go make something happen. *Right now*.

DATE

GIVE ME SOME FEED BACK ON
WHERE TO GO WITH THIS.

ONE WORD / TWO WORDS
SAK WITH A "K"
LESS / MORE COLOR
LETTERS

THE NAME

October 1998. I finally give in to my neighbor's pleadings and decide to make them a Sac like mine as a Christmas present for their kids. I've been busy with college, jobs to pay my way through school, and volunteer work over the past three years and I have lots of irons in the fire. So if I'm going to take the time to make and *sell* these things, then I'm going to need a business ... and if I need a business, then I'm going to need a name. Love, peace, hate, war, hippie, beanbag—that 1970s vibe—peace bag, love bag ... love sack.

Ahhhhhhh—I like that.

I pay twenty-five bucks to register with the Utah State tax commission, and "Lovesac" is born. (I don't like K's; they feel cheap to me.)

I utilize the same, painstaking foam-chopping methods to fill that second Sac, and I'm reminded why I never made another one in the first place. Three weeks of chopping is not sustainable. But my neighbors love their finished Sac, and the word is out. Their friends want one, and *their* friends want one ...

My artistic high school buddy, Herb, is staying over, on holiday leave from his station with the Coast Guard in Hawaii. I buy him a fresh pack of Magic Markers and tell him I need a logo, explaining how I came up with the name, and how "Lovesac" is meant to be the ultimate retro-chill vibe, embodying that fun, happy, hippie-love lifestyle. He fishes a piece of scratch planner paper out of the desk in my room and goes to work.

I roll out some more vinyl on the floor of my mother's retired dance studio in the basement. I tape a Sharpie marker to a string and tie a small knot in it at the other end. I kneel on the knot, and I stretch it out taut to draw the arcs of the figure-eight Sac patterns on the backside of the fabric. I cut them out on the floor with kitchen scissors. I can't possibly find enough beanbag beads for this beast. I'll need loads of foam to chop up for fill. What has foam? Sofa cushions! I search in our Yellow Pages phone book (no Google back then!) for furniture factories in the area and I find one downtown.

I just keep doing the *next thing*.

I JUST KEEP DOING THE *NEXT THING.*

They're willing to sell me the foam scraps off their shop floor if I show up, sweep up, and bag it up myself each week. I haul it home and cut it into strips on the paper cutter, then chop it the other way, same as I did for the first Sac. It takes weeks. I'm two months in and five Sacs along before the lady at the front desk mentions, as I'm paying for a load of foam one day, that they have a dormant shredding machine in back I could perhaps resurrect. It's in the farthest corner. They haven't touched it in years.

I enlist my father to help me get this 1970s-era contraption running again. It's like a backyard wood chipper but powered by an industrial electric motor in need of rewinding and repair. My dad helps me get it rebuilt. We use kitchen knives, right from my mother's drawer, to cut the larger pieces of foam down into small enough strips to fit into the orange machine's metal mouth for pulverizing.

My first college-buddy-employee accidentally slices off the tip of his thumb with the knife one day while stuffing. He calls me from the hospital where, thankfully, they've stitched it back together. The nurses are interrogating him as to whether this accident happened "on the job." "Where do you work? Who is your boss? What is their insurance carrier?"

I receive a menacing letter from the State of Utah not long after. I'm sick to my stomach just looking at the official state seal on the envelope. I feel so dumb. I feel so broke. I feel so *bad*.

I've disfigured my friend's thumb, and now I've learned the hard way what workers' comp insurance is.

JUST DO THE NEXT THING

Business, plans, finance, accounting, legal, insurance, supply, structure, strategy—it can all seem so demanding and complex. Most of the time, however, you just need to do the next thing, and then the next, and then the next, and the next again. It's not rocket science. Build a team eventually, and you can do many next-things. The key, as with most contact sports, is to maintain forward momentum. Don't stop for anything. If you're going to fall, fall forward.

In college, I kept cranking out Sacs, and it was pretty cool to be the only kid in my college accounting and economics courses who could fully relate to the concepts being discussed in real time. The number of problems and deficiencies with my tiny business already felt overwhelming, embarrassing, even insurmountable.

Over many years, The Lovesac Company would grow into a billion-dollar publicly traded corporation with thousands of employees. This is not something that seemed remotely possible or even relevant to me until decades in. I was just trying to survive and keep it alive because ... it was fun!

There are not enough pages in any book to recount all of the steps, hurdles, plans, realities, difficulties, systems, procedures, forms, licenses, relationships, contracts, hires, projects, processes, culture, capabilities, consultants, and ideas that got us here. It wouldn't be useful to you if I did. But I *can* tell you that *all* things are possible. There is *nothing* you can't do, whether it involves starting a business or just getting to that next level in your own job or hobby. The Lovesac saga is living proof of this. That even with all of the inevitable shortcomings and mistakes, with a bit of luck and a few miracles along the way, you'll see the universe unfold before you.

WITH A BIT OF LUCK AND A FEW MIRACLES ALONG THE WAY, YOU'LL SEE THE UNIVERSE UNFOLD BEFORE YOU.

Sometimes, if we're willing to just take that next step, and the next one again no matter how small, before long we're able to look back on how far we've come and surprise even ourselves with what has been accomplished. Pick up the phone. Make that uncomfortable phone call—right now. Ask the dumb question. Write down the idea, connection, or contact right now. Make the sketch. Draw up the plan. Send the email. Then just do that *next* thing—and the one after that. In each case, at every stage, and in any situation, even a very average person like me can figure out how to move things forward, strive, and, eventually, thrive because I always just did *that next thing*. And so can you.

THE LAWN

May 1999. Their friends want one. Now their friends want one, and *their* friends want one ... Lovesac is my side hustle in college as I try to balance dual tracks at the University of Utah in Chinese and Business. The work is not glamorous: cutting out Sacs on my hands and knees, sweeping scrap foam off the factory floor, cutting it up, shredding, stuffing, cleaning, loading, delivering.

We deal with broken gears, broken blades, jammed-up shafts, burnt-out motors, electrical fires, and—finally—a few friends, willing to work for free as business partners, helping me keep up. Maybe we'll actually get somewhere someday with this Lovesac thing—maybe we'll make some real money—who knows?

Our first formal sales event is on the lawn outside of the student union building at the university during its annual "May Fest" event. We set up a folding table, photocopied brochures, a three-ring binder full of blank order forms, and play Bob Marley on a battery-powered boombox. Toss one of each size Sac on the lawn, and let's see what happens.

It's a party. Everybody loves it. That same reliable Lovesac effect—love at first sit. Some are even willing to pay the few hundred bucks for a giant not-beanbag, just to take a little piece of that Lovesac vibe back to their own home, dorm room, or frat house. Lovesac is as much a vibe as it is a product.

To our surprise, some even want our T-shirts. Mostly, though, we take a small deposit, write down the size and color of their choosing, and spend the next few weeks making a Sac for them.

Registration, preparation, sample-making, load-in, setup, all-day demonstrating. Tear down, take home, order process, draw-out, cut-out, drop-off at the seamstress's house. Pick up, shred, stuff, deliver, collect, deposit, repeat.

That is the work required for every boat show, car show, beer fest, and Christmas Expo that drives our silly side hustle called Lovesac in year number one. My best friend since junior high (so obviously my first choice as a business partner), Christian, recommends James, who is "studying marketing" in school, to join the team. There's *three* of us now, willing to sweep floors, unload, pick up, or do whatever needs doing for *free* ... alongside school, our social lives, and our "real jobs" that actually pay money.

We have no idea it will be *years* before we will ever see a dime from any of this.

BE WILLING TO SWEEP FLOORS

There is nothing too hard, too long, too complicated, or too low for you. It doesn't matter how big the organization gets or how long you've been at it. It doesn't matter your title, your tenure, your education, your career, or to what degree you may have already "paid your dues." You are *always* willing to do whatever it takes. You are even willing to sweep the floors if that's what needs doing.

On the other hand, as things get more sophisticated, jobs become more specialized, and you necessarily take on new responsibilities. This "willing to sweep floors attitude" doesn't mean that you always *will* sweep floors. It is probably not the best use of your time and abilities to do so. The principle is a matter of never losing the sincere *willingness* to do it—and, when your back's against the wall, do it with a smile. There must certainly arise more efficient methods to get the sweeping done, even *as* we propel forward our more ambitious strategies. But preserving this attitude is critical to maintaining your edge, bolstering your credibility, and keeping a finger on the pulse of what's *really* going on in an organization.

And what of getting ahead? Everybody wants to be promoted. Everyone wants to "make the big bucks." You want to "show them what you're capable of." How is this achieved? First, make sure you are on the right bus. If your ambitions greatly exceed the size or scope of the organization ("the bus") you've chosen to ride on, then your opportunities there will be limited out of the gate. Consider a different bus. Second, make sure the people you report to and those above them are *good* people with honest intentions. Seek to work with A-players. If they are, then they will recognize and reward strong talent. Merit will guide their decisions. If they are not good, honest A-players (or at least striving to become such), then their decisions will reek of politics, nepotism, ego, or fear. You're on the wrong bus with the wrong people.

The third piece is the linchpin, and it is simple: Just be awesome. Be *amazing*. Be an A-player. Exceed expectations. If you are truly awesome at whatever it is you're doing, like the best one—or in the top 5 percent maybe—you will be noticed, you will be recognized, and eventually granted more pay, responsibility, and opportunity. On the *right* bus with good people, you can ultimately climb as high as your capabilities and attitude will allow.

As a person who has been hiring others for decades, I can tell you: truly awesome people do not grow on trees. And it's not just about being awesome *at that job*. To gain the advancement you seek, you need to be awesome *all around*. This means that on top of your stellar work ethic and consistently excellent results you are a positive, flexible, sharp, passionate, friendly, empathetic, loyal, teachable and polished person. You exhibit all of the other good traits you'd want to see in the people who might work for *you*. It's pretty straightforward really, but most of us are not honest enough with *ourselves* to recognize where we fall short. Or sometimes we're just unwilling to pay the price, so we don't change. *Self-awareness is the key* to unlocking awesomeness.

Finally, as I've said to so many around me along the way, *be patient*. This can be an off-putting message to people with ambition. But infinite patience is required to achieve audacious goals.

As you progress in your career and take on new responsibilities, seek the opportunity to *do* some of the front-line or back-line work occasionally. I spend time working in Lovesac stores, and in the factories. Stay grounded. Stay connected to and grateful for the people who do the work you used to do or the work that supports you now. They are every bit as human and worthy of respect as *you* are. They are every bit as important to the organization. Remember the foundational lesson: love matters.

Never lose your *willingness* to sweep floors, both metaphorically and literally, and you will become a uniquely effective leader, known for your integrity.

"STAY GROUNDED. STAY CONNECTED TO AND GRATEFUL FOR THE PEOPLE WHO DO THE WORK YOU USED TO DO OR THE WORK THAT SUPPORTS YOU NOW."

THE FIFTY

March 2000. I'm in my third year at university. I'm dating this really cool architecture major, Christie, who happens to be a part-time Red Bull promoter. She drives around in that little silver and blue car with a giant Red Bull can-shaped cooler on the back of it, handing out samples all day.

I ask her, "With all of the events and competitions Red Bull is involved with, do you think they could use a few Sacs for the athletes or onlookers to lounge on as part of their event staging?"

She reminds me that Red Bull is a multibillion-dollar, worldwide organization, and she is not even a full-time employee there.

"Well, you never know until you ask," I prod.

A miracle. The ensuing order for fifty silver and blue vinyl Supersacs is more work than we have ever seen ... and it lands on the eve of me necessarily departing to China for a student-work internship that would last a year. My parents, who are thoroughly entertained by the scrappy furniture empire spontaneously growing out of the old dance studio in the basement, allow Dave, Janke, Tres, and all my friends and partners to come and go as necessary in order to hopefully keep Lovesac alive until I get back from China.

Good luck.

LESSON #4

YOU NEVER KNOW UNTIL YOU ASK

There are always a hundred excuses to hold back, be shy, feel embarrassed, or shrink because of doubt. Most desired outcomes remain unfulfilled wishes or dreams unless you're bold enough to *ask* for them. Over these decades, I can think of a hundred times that I needed a sale just to make ends meet or investment dollars in the thousands, millions, or even tens of millions, which seemed unfathomable to me at the time, until I was forced to find a way. I did the necessary work to prepare, and I *made the ask*.

I can think of at least a dozen different times that to level up, I would need to compel a new potential business partner or employee to make the very personal decision to abandon their fancy career and come on board to join little Lovesac. We could pay some fraction of their previous salary and offer few to no benefits comparatively. I was sure it would be impossible— even humiliating—to expect of them. I recognized, and tried to be totally transparent about, the personal risk they might be taking by joining me. But

I made the ask anyway. In almost each case, I've been surprised and grateful when the answer would eventually get to "yes."

Whether raising money to grow a business or reaching out to attract top talent, remember: *You* have the opportunity for *them*. Be unapologetic. Both exercises can be humbling and loaded with disappointment. Both may require many rounds and much rejection. Just power through and seek until you find. It will be way harder than you first imagined.

Carve up equity and ownership as conservatively and as *late* as possible, balancing your need for great talent. Keep titles generally as *low* as possible at the outset so there is room to grow. Compensation and job titles can always be expanded but are almost impossible to unwind. Over time, be as generous as you can be in sharing the wealth. It is much more satisfying and effective to have a team of great people pulling together to grow your pie larger than it is to hoard a smaller pie for yourself. Selfishness may be lucrative but is ultimately lonely.

Don't compare your exact compensation or situation with others too closely either. As Teddy Roosevelt supposedly said, "Comparison is the thief of joy." There are all kinds of crazy examples of people in the right place at the right time, depending on circumstance and context. You never know their full story though, and I've learned that given enough time, I wouldn't trade my situation for any of theirs—even the ones who have made piles of money faster or seemingly easier than I have.

Focus on winning over the long run. Be realistic about your *own* value in the market, respectful of the context and your investors, partners, and team as well. Advocate strongly for yourself along the way but only when you are certain it is justified. Timing is everything. Choose your shots well. Business can be shrewd, and nobody is going to offer any handouts. Always stay grateful for what you *do* have—even as you chase your top ambitions.

But make the ask. You never know until you ask.

THE CLIENT

March 2001. I'm back from my year working in China just in time to wrap up my final semester at university. I'm finally going to shut down this money-losing time-sucking side hustle called Lovesac. At twenty-four years old I'm looking forward to the high-paying international consulting job now waiting for me back in Shanghai with the firm I had just successfully interned with. I need to get these final few Sacs that Red Bull ordered a year ago shrunken down and shipped out. That same order I took before I left is still not complete! This characterizes just how dinky our silly foam bag business still is, even three years in.

Customers and friends aware of our intentions protest, "You can't just close Lovesac—we *love* our Lovesacs." We hesitate. We decide to give it one last shot. I charge around $15,000 of expenses to my credit card to attend an industry trade show in Chicago. We're hoping to land some big orders similar to the one we just completed for Red Bull—or bust. The biggest companies in the United States attend this show in search of new promotional product ideas and innovations. All the big buyers laugh, same as always, as they flop down in one of our Sacs with a big smile on their face—but none of them can make sense of what to do with it. It's a bust.

I'm back in the corner of the borrowed downtown Salt Lake City warehouse shredding foam and stuffing a few final Sacs for friends when my phone rings. It's an out-of-state number. I shut off the shredder, brushing the foam dust out of my hair as the motor winds down. I answer very professionally, "Lovesac Corporation."

On the line is a buyer at one of these huge retail chains who saw our booth at the show, fell into a Sac one time, and couldn't get it out of their head. They're ready to order 12,000 little Sacs in time for the holidays from us. I assure them, "We're the best not-beanbag company in the world, so 12,000 units is no problem." I hang up the phone and get to work asking around to find the fabric the client requires at the ridiculously low price they've demanded for this kind of volume. They have no idea our company is really just me, a couple of buddies, a 1979 Dodge Van, and a borrowed shredder. We are, in fact at this time, the *only* not-beanbag company in the world, and therefore the best—just as I told them.

But we have no idea how to pull this off.

"THEY HAVE NO IDEA OUR COMPANY IS REALLY JUST ME, A COUPLE OF BUDDIES, A 1979 DODGE VAN, AND A BORROWED SHREDDER."

BE WHAT YOU WILL BE, NOT WHAT YOU ARE

Your business, your career, your reputation—you're always becoming *something*, so act like *that*. Put on the clothes (metaphorically speaking), use the language, and adopt the mentality of what it is you intend to become, rather than just default to whatever you currently *are*. Learn to communicate well and listen actively. Look people right in the eye. Learn to exude confidence. Confidence is free.

Practice speaking, conducting meetings, performing, and leading teams or projects with every chance you get—even if it's awkward at first. Consider how you are perceived by others—shape those perceptions. How you dress, how you act, how you speak, and especially how you make people *feel*. Don't just leave it all to chance, hiding behind the overused mantra, "Well, this is just who I am." We are all constantly evolving, and it's okay to evolve deliberately rather than by default.

This requires effort, self-awareness, discipline, and intention. First, identify the core principles, values, and key attributes that are authentic to *you*. Write them down. Stay true to those so that you *can* be your authentic self, even as you thoughtfully shape how you come across to others on the outside. It is not about trying to live up to some traditional standard of refinement or professionalism. Imagine the kind of person you want to become. Visualize it with great detail. Write down the characteristics of successful role models you might aspire to, then blend those characteristics with the core attributes that are unique to your own personality and style.

When that pivotal call came through for me (and you never know when that moment might arrive, so be ready), I was a credit-card-debt-ridden, not-yet-college-graduate, part-time waiter living in my parents' basement. I had zero big business experience.

But on the phone with that buyer, I chose to *be* the CEO of the "greatest not-beanbag company in the world." I spoke that way, I acted that way, I dressed that way when it mattered—and most importantly, I *believed* that way in order to *make* it true.

This same strategy would prove useful a hundred times over across the next few decades on our path toward a billion and beyond. I continue to evolve who I am and what I am becoming with loyalty only to my core unchanging principles and values because I know what they are and I protect them. The rest is a choice. Have fun with it.

Be what you *will be*, not what you are.

THE FABRIC

April 2001. I fly to High Point, North Carolina, to attend the largest fabric show in North America. I'm in search of the elusive blue-furry-fabric-with-little-silver-specs-in-it that my client demands to complete their 12,000 Sacs order. I buy a blue dress shirt at Banana Republic, don it over my Lovesac T-shirt, and tuck it into my khaki cargo pants trying my best to look the part of a not-just-a-college-kid-snowboarder, but a young professional. I walk the largest convention center I've ever seen top to bottom. I finally discover the fabric they want after half a day searching, but it is twice the price I need to make the deal work for the customer.

The crusty fabric dealer rejects any attempt to negotiate. "I'm a direct importer ... you're not going to find it any cheaper you know." I'm about to give up on the entire business once again, cut my losses, and return to enjoy my college graduation and the long overdue shuttering of this weighted-anchor-of-a-business called Lovesac, still dragging me down further into debt.

I think, "How can this middle-class-raised-student-waiter possibly even find the cash to *buy* the thirty thousand yards of fabric necessary to make this order, even if the fabric *were* affordable?"

I'M SATISFIED TO HAVE AT LEAST "TRIED." BUT I CAN'T QUIT JUST YET.

As I turn to leave the show, I'm satisfied to have at least "tried." I can now shut Lovesac down in peace knowing that I gave it my best. But I can't quit just yet. I can't help but notice the Chinese writing printed on the side of each trade show sample box that is stacked up in the corner of this man's disheveled fabric booth as I'm walking away. I'm a month away from graduating with a degree in Mandarin Chinese. I've spent two years in Taiwan fully immersed in it as a volunteer missionary for my church and another year in Shanghai delivering leadership courses in Mandarin to Fortune 500 executives there.

Thankfully, I can read the Chinese writing on these boxes, unbeknownst to the ancient bushy-eyebrowed agent trying to squeeze me for a quick profit. It is the address of the fabric mill in China that actually *makes* this fabric. I can't *not* go down this rabbit hole. I can't *not* do the next thing. Reluctantly, I book *another* flight back to Shanghai to see where it leads.

But first, being on my first trip ever to the East Coast, I utilize the balance of the second day with a rental car that I paid good money for, to road-trip up Washington, D.C. All alone, I visit our nation's capital and the monuments I've seen before only in pictures. I read the plaques and take the tours. I see a reenactment of a Revolutionary War battle.

I am impressed with the low-rise blocky architecture and symmetrical layout of the city, in contrast to Chicago, where I was just a few weeks prior. All of this is new and exciting. Each new place offers a fresh point of view on the world. It's easy to miss if we're moving too fast to take it in. My understanding of our country, the world, business, and people is expanding at breakneck speed. Returning to the drudgery of waiting tables in Utah will be difficult, but necessary.

But first, I'm off to China again...

BE AN INSATIABLE LEARNER

I'm not one of these entrepreneurs telling you to drop out of school and chase your dreams. I loved my time at university—not the classes I was required to take for my degree, but the ones that I *chose* to take for the purpose of *learning*. I loved the whole social experience, however awkward it was at times. College was fun—and there is value in that. I consider it part of the "education," and I encourage it for anyone with ambition. Perhaps it's because I'm not naturally gifted or smart or talented, in any particular way. I don't write code. I don't know finance. Perhaps it's because my parents, thankfully, drummed into my brain the idea that "we keep our commitments, do our absolute best, and *always* finish what we start." I graduated with honors.

But education in any form is critical and should be an endless pursuit. We can choose to fill the seams and cracks of our lives with books, podcasts, classes, and courses over empty entertainment only. We can travel. We can get a passport and leave the country. As a nineteen-year-old missionary in Taiwan, I would wake up an hour earlier than the already rigid 6:00 a.m. requirement, just to cram in that extra time for Chinese study, over and above the scheduled study time. I did this for two years, relentlessly. I became totally fluent. Most missionaries return home *speaking* well enough, but are unable to read or write the Chinese characters like I can. I couldn't have possibly known at the time how this hard-earned skill would pay off down the road for me.

Read, read, read. More important than the words on the page are the thoughts and impressions you will have as you are exposed to concepts and ideas found in books and articles. The thoughts that materialize while reading can be especially poignant when we are actively engaged in a challenging pursuit or working on a problem. Write your inspirations down. All of my books, to this day, are littered with underlines, circles, and notes to myself in the margins. Let these thoughts that come "between the lines" shape your thinking and strategy. Put them to use.

Network, network, network. Say "yes" to events and activities where you can meet new people. Connections lead to more connections so get out. Be bold enough to seek out people who are experts in their field and ask them endless questions. Be curious. Be humble enough to learn something from *anybody*—even those we do not like or those we compete with. We can learn a great deal from those who are younger or those in positions of less power than we are. But it takes humility. *All* people have something to offer. There are ways we can learn from them, even if sometimes it's how *not* to behave.

Seek to become a total pro in *something* and become generally knowledgeable across many areas. All information is available to us now via the internet, but we must exercise some discipline to seek it out, take it in, and connect the dots across all dimensions as they overlap. Art, literature, science, math, music, languages, economics, finance, design, health, relationships, management, leadership. Knowledge builds upon knowledge. It can all be accretive. Invest in yourself consistently over the long haul, and experience and wisdom will emerge.

Be an insatiable learner—and *never* stop.

THE MILL

May 2001. I fly fifteen hours in coach. Jet-lagged and nervous, I enter the downtown Shanghai skyscraper sales office representing this Chinese fabric mill. Butterflies. I use English—not wanting to show all my cards yet. Referring to the client's fabric clipping, I explain that we need thirty thousand yards of this blue-furry-fabric-with-little-silver-specs-in-it. The broken-English-speaking sales team takes the sample from my hand, turning it in their fingers to assess its weight. First, quoting me the same price as their agent in America, this factory team begins discussing the fabric's specifications and production process in Mandarin, right in front of me. I understand it all. Now I *know* they can hit my price.

I negotiate for days, using only English, but I'm able to understand all of their side conversations in Chinese. They finally capitulate and meet my uncannily accurate price-per-meter demands. Call it a win! Then they say casually, "We'll just need a $65,000 deposit to begin milling the fabric."

With no money to make the required deposit, I return to my cheap hotel and dial up my retail-juggernaut client. I inform them, "I am at my factory in China, ready to build your order. I am going to need a $65,000 deposit to begin production."

They're too large and reputable. They're beyond offering deposits to their suppliers for orders they place. But after much arm-twisting, I convince them to wire me the money anyway. "Lovesac has never done a deal without a deposit, what's wrong with you?" I protest, not untruthfully. The wire will have to go to my University of Utah Credit Union checking account for Lovesac. It's all I've got. Thankfully, they don't seem to question it. I wire the money to my new factory partner. I've now spent the client's money, and the clock is ticking. I'm committed.

I conveniently pay a visit to the twenty-fourth floor of the famous Isetan office-building high-rise nearby in downtown Shanghai, where I had worked the previous summer as a paid intern for "Pro Way," an international leadership development firm run by this hulking expatriate Ph.D. from Oklahoma named Gene. He is a former U.S. consul general. An outlandishly high-paying leadership role awaits me now at Pro Way. It's my dream job, really. It's an exceptional opportunity for this new college graduate to live overseas and travel throughout Asia, in business class, flexing my language skills and my penchant for public speaking and performance.

I take the long ride up the elevator and walk inside smiling nervously with all kinds of conflicted and confused anxiety. We celebrate our reunion and my unlikely surprise visit from across the world. My time there over the previous year was exciting, fun, and lucrative for me and for their firm. I had quickly become a key part of their team. My Chinese is better than any of their foreign staff. They've looked forward to my return having offered me a leadership position after graduation.

After the pleasantries, I inform Gene that I won't be able to take his job offer after all. He bites his lip and expels a long, loud breath from his nose, as he does. He is apparently disappointed—but he is like a big teddy bear and has become a mentor of mine. We talk it out.

"Beanbags? Really?"

He gives me a big bear hug to say goodbye. Thankfully, I survive it and skulk out, conflicted.

I now have 12,000 not-beanbags in need of stuffing on their way, with the promise of working for free yet again for the next six months at least while we stuff them. I fly back home with a pit in my stomach and a mass of instant regret.

I need to somehow materialize an industrial-scale Sac-*stuffing* facility out of thin air.

PUSH YOURSELF OUT OF THE NEST

It was really the transfer of my client's deposit funds from my account to the fabric mill that put my back up against the wall. Not to mention the mounting stack of credit-card debt that was racking up interest and could not be ignored. There comes a point though, before any major change in your career, business, or personal life, where you can greatly improve your odds for good outcomes by making a bold decision to *ditch the safety net*. Push yourself out of the nest. Embrace the economic pressure. There is almost nothing more powerful than the desperate weight of financial burden to drive innovation.

It had already been almost three years since founding Lovesac as a company, but it had never been more than a side hustle for me. I had backup plan upon backup plan as musician, waiter, handyman, and, most recently, suit-wearing international leadership training consultant to Fortune 500 companies in Shanghai.

For anything to become more than a hobby, shot-in-the-dark side hustle, or distraction, it will require total commitment at some point. The key is to leave those safety nets in place for as long as possible, but intuitively find your way to the right moment, recognize when it's time to fully commit, then go for it! Be brave. Both feet in. Don't look back.

It can be the same with projects inside an organization. Sometimes big initiatives require being "pushed out of the nest" by taking some kind of action that really commits you and forces the organization to move forward. New, big initiatives need to be highly scrutinized and broadly aligned for sure. But by virtue of their heft and inherent risk, sometimes we have a hard time moving these ideas past the planning and debate stage. After an appropriate amount of consideration, just buy the equipment, place the order, sign the (well-vetted) contract, hit send, take the job, quit the job, or make the hire. Just do *something* that obliges you to move forward and makes it hard to turn back.

You will never be totally certain, and it will continue to be scary, even as it unfolds. But make that commitment and ignore the temptation to entertain the "what if" worst-case scenarios that haunt you. Turn them off. Compartmentalize. Move ahead without second-guessing. You've pushed yourself out of the nest, now you must *make* it work, as if your life depends on it.

By the way—if you really *do* take one moment to honestly contemplate your *actual* worst-case scenario should you get it wrong, it's probably not as bad as you think. Many of us might just end up fired, couch surfing, or back in our parents' basement or garage—alone or with our families—or worse, with our in-laws. So what?

After enough really *fabulous* things happen to you in this life, along with some really *terrible* things as well, you come to a point where you realize that *nobody really cares* anyway! We post our best and sometimes worst occasions on social media. We get likes and shares and comments and then … there is a funny cat video. Nobody cares! Get over it. You're on your own, and you'll be left on your own to sort things out if the worst ever actually does come to pass. But that *still* likely beats death or dismemberment. Most "huge" decisions that we end up stressing out about or losing sleep over do not actually carry life-and-death stakes with them anyway.

Be bold. Be brave. Make a move. Push yourself out of the nest.

THE HAYBUSTER

June 2001. I now must conjure up a factory to shred, stuff, clean, shrink, box, stack, and wrap every one of these blue furry Sacs once they arrive. *There is always a way.* I apply for every credit-card offer I can get my hands on, all on the same day, to game the system. This effort funds a cash advance straight from the ATM for our deposit and first month's rent on a lease for a larger empty warehouse space next to the borrowed building with our original electric shredder inside.

Exploring every possible way to process an estimated 250,000 pounds of scrap foam into popcorn-sized pieces, we find our way three hours out of town into farm country, where they deal in heavy equipment. After looking at a few small shredders like the one we're familiar with, I'm shown a gargantuan, well-worn machine from the 1980s called a "Haybuster," which is powered by a direct-driveline PTO (power take-off) from the back of a full-size farm tractor.

Three hours back to town to retrieve a truck bed full of scrap foam. Three hours back out to the farm. The first giant bag of foam we throw into the Haybuster bogs and clogs the machine instantly. The tractor is stalled—silent. We're devastated. The farmer, shaking his head, can't believe his eyes. He's seen this thing pulverize wooden beams to sawdust. But, after four more visits and some scrappy on-site modifications to account for the stretch in the foam, this clumsy machine just might do the job.

I apply for an agricultural loan from the U.S. government for farm equipment. The flatbed trailer bearing our vintage Haybuster and accompanying tractor is delivered to the parking lot in front of our newly leased downtown Salt Lake City warehouse space. The Haybuster can sit just inside the loading-dock door. It will convey shredded foam onto a huge netted table with holes in it through which we can stuff the Sacs. But the tractor must remain outside the building as its loud diesel engine produces heat and exhaust. We have it hoisted onto a low scaffold meant to elevate it to the height of a loading dock, so it can provide a direct connection to the shredder via PTO.

It ain't pretty, but now we have the capacity to shred, literally, *tons* of foam.

THERE IS ALWAYS A WAY

No truer statement exists. It doesn't matter what the problem is. It doesn't matter what industry, category, situation, subject matter, project, or profession. There may be compromises and trade-offs required, there may be a price to pay, but there is *always a way*. If it has been done, it *can* be done. If someone else has done it, then why not me? When faced with *any* challenge, no matter how large, we must first tamp down our natural responses of fear and anxiety. These will inevitably attempt to overwhelm us. The more this tamping down becomes a habit, the more we can become unflappable—not easily rattled by *anything* in *any* realm on *any* day. No fear. That is the goal.

Only play to win. With maximum effort and a winning attitude consistent through the preparation stages and up until the last minute of the "game," the *only* acceptable attitude is: *We will win this.* End of story. All players experience defeat … but defeat is never an option until it has finally arrived. There is always a way. That is the attitude.

Now get busy solving the problem. Use your imagination. To this day, I literally find a quiet place, a comfortable couch, a Sac, or a bed, and I'll just lay there and *think*—mostly with my eyes closed. The trick is to not fall asleep. But I can spend hours alone in deep concentration, just imagining and reimagining solutions to problems.

Design problems. Engineering problems. Relationship problems. Financial problems. Management problems. Business problems. Form a hypothesis, conceive of a solution, and then pressure-test it from every angle, all in your mind. This costs nothing, but it does require significant focus, time, and energy. Build it. Challenge it. Tear it down. Rebuild it a different way. Visualize it from every angle. Try to disprove it. Try to make it fail. Reimagine failed solutions that have been long dismissed by experts in times past, repairing their flaws to be tested anew.

Explore even the most preposterous solutions that logical people would dismiss outright due to their obvious implausibility or ridiculousness. The craziest ones can often lead us down sideways paths to the places where the most novel ideas grow. Make notes of the most useful inspirations that emerge. Don't lose them. Go try it out now in real life. Prototype. Expand the process to others. Brainstorm. Ask people what they think. Don't be shy. Try things on.

Test your crazy ideas out verbally with *lots* of people, diverse groups of people, abandoning all ego or embarrassment. Let them think you're ridiculous. Remember, *nobody cares!* Ask the smartest people you know. Ask the most unassuming people you know. No one has a corner on the market for good ideas—they can come from anywhere and anyone. Everything comes at a cost, and you may, ultimately, decide you are unwilling to pay the price. Compromises are usually necessary, something always gives. But *everything* is possible.

There is always a way.

THE SEMI

September 2001. We open the giant hinged metal doors and feel the weight of what's ahead. It is shocking to behold just how many tightly packed boxes full of neatly folded furry blue Sac covers from China will fit on a forty-foot-long ocean container once it arrives. We unload it by hand.

Gratefully, Christian, James, Dan, Jon, Tres, Oly, Sherri, Cheri, and many other friends have been showing up to help us build the place, volunteer, and assist where they can. Dave is one of these, and he quickly becomes my most reliable sidekick. He's still working his "day job" too so we don't have to support him on the payroll yet. He's a loader at UPS, which begins at 2:00 a.m. each morning.

We build shop tables for cleaning, high-pressure vacuums for shrinking, make Haybuster modifications, and construct the giant netted table meant to consolidate shredded foam for stuffing. We line the table where the workers will lean against it with some of our leopard velvet Sac fabric. This is in a conscious effort to make every detail of our fledgling company, brand, and factory a bit remark-able (unique enough to elicit a remark from someone) wherever we can.

At 5:00 a.m. the next day I'm at a nearby gas station filling up four red cans with diesel fuel in the dark. By 6:00 a.m. the tractor usually starts and is warming up as the early shift arrives each frosty fall morning. We have a few partners, a few employees, some friends, and a bunch of temp laborers speaking three different languages.

Dave usually shows up after his other job halfway through our first run, and we work shoulder-to-shoulder with temp laborers over two long shifts each day, well into the night. Some are loading foam into the Haybuster, clumsily unclogging it from time to time when big chunks get stuck and cause the tractor to stall. Others stand around the netted table stuffing Sacs by hand. Some blow off and clean these plump, furry static-magnets before bagging and shrinking them for packing, while others build boxes, tape them, load them, and stack them.

We use ladders to build the thirteen-foot-tall palletized stacks, lined up and ready to load by forklift onto what will be the first of five full truckloads we'll need to ship out over the next few weeks to meet the deadline. We take turns holding a roll of industrial shrink-wrap while balanced on a shipping pallet up in the air as the other drives the forklift around in circles to wrap and secure the neatly stacked boxes.

A screaming match ensues between me and the dispatcher at the trucking company toward the end of our first week of production. None of our twenty-four carefully shrink-wrapped pallets will fit onto what is clearly "a non-standard semi-trailer."

"Oh wait, you meant the trucks are thirteen feet tall when measuring up from the *ground below*?"

My mistake. I am mortified. I am an idiot. I am scrambling.

We must now dismantle every pallet-load from the first week and make them much shorter just to fit into the semi. We have to schedule two extra semi-truckloads that we hadn't budgeted for as well. This is how inexperienced all of us are. Worse, this is emblematic of how inefficient the entire process would turn out to be. It's one of a hundred reasons we are doomed to make no money on this gigantic order, our hands stained blue already, just two weeks into what will be an eight-week grind. Not to mention, when 9/11 happens in week two, the price of foam then goes up on us, as does the cost of freight. We now have only a glimmer of hope to break even on the whole endeavor.

I'm physically, mentally, emotionally, and financially broken as we close the door on the seventh and final truckload on October 19th, just in time for our client's holiday delivery cutoff.

Now what?

GRIT IS HALF THE GAME

Building anything to scale is just plain hard. It is complex and multifaceted. But if you need *one* trait to succeed in the end, it is *this* one. True grit can make up for almost any deficiency. In the early stages, the grit it takes to succeed is often physical and emotional. Over time and with scale, challenges become more unyielding, escaping the bounds where even the relentless tenacity and hard work of an entire team cannot guarantee success. The necessary fortitude then shifts to the mental, intellectual, and disciplined sort of grit—but it is grit, nonetheless.

Grit at scale is more than just doggedness. It is the rigor to work proactively to seek out talent and establish an environment where talent can thrive. The grit to not just fix a problem in the moment but to dig in deep and establish a process to fix that *type* of problem in perpetuity, in a replicable and scalable way. The grit to dig in with some stubbornness to defend our strongest instincts, paired with the humility to maintain an open mind and let others solve things, even with styles and solutions that may be very different from our own.

The grit to wake up a little earlier to study or to get fit or both. The self-control to say "*no*" to exciting and obvious projects that can certainly bear fruit—but come as a distraction to more primary goals. "Do less, and do best," a guiding principle at Lovesac today, can grow to feel like a real drag when there are so many cool new things we could do right now so "easily" if we just chose to. It requires grit to stay focused and see things all the way through before shifting our attention—however long it takes.

On the flip side, you need grit to swallow your pride, reverse course, and admit when you have made the wrong choice or have been rowing in the wrong direction once it becomes apparent—however damaging to your own ego it may be. The grit to prioritize projects and prune the team with intellectual honesty, based on facts and research—listening to customers and really *hearing* what they need, versus hoping blindly that they find your own ideas to be as brilliant as you do.

The grit to bite your lip—to not *always* say what you think or drive to a verbal victory at the expense of your team's trust. Sit back and observe more. Be an ear to someone's problems, criticism, or to a good debate. Often, this is all that is required. People typically say things they don't mean as they struggle to express their own nagging instincts. We can sometimes be too quick to react, argue, and force our own agendas. This pushes others into a corner to defend their emergent positions, and before you know it, you've wasted much energy on circular arguments that go nowhere or, worse, can unintentionally provoke damaging dialogue.

Early on, as a young CEO, I would get wind of a debate or disagreement between two leaders within the organization or maybe a brewing discussion that ran in direct contrast to my own initiative. I would pull the offenders into my office and, in the name of transparency and candor, try to solve their issues with them. After countless unproductive conversations I finally realized that *people just need to complain* sometimes. It's okay. Let it happen. Hear what they have to say if you are privy to it. Consider it. Let it roll off and ignore it if it isn't meant for your ears. Exercise the grit to wait for it to be developed enough and brought *to* you as a more useful challenge. Or allow it to just fizzle out, as most do, when people are allowed the space to process.

Just because people have something to say, even if it's negative, doesn't mean they are undermining you—they're just doing what people do.

Grit, in all its forms, is a crucial attribute of champions. Grit is half the game.

THE MALL

November 2001. What an idiot. I've been so desperately focused on completing this twelve thousand Sac order that, when we come up for air at the end of October, we have rent due on our warehouse space, equipment loan payments, and workers who want to keep working, but we have *no* new customers to sell to. We scramble, taking our new solution for fully shrunken giant foam Sacs, now with removable, washable, and change-able covers, to the arrogant merchandise buyers at the biggest furniture retail chains in the West.

We are rejected, full stop. No furniture store wants to sell our products.

"Nobody is going to pay $500 for a beanbag chair—certainly not with *that* ridiculous brand name embroidered on it."

I should have kept *one hand on the now, and one hand on the next.* Instead, both of mine are *still* stained blue, cracked and bleeding now from personally stuffing and packaging many hundreds of them myself, to complete the 12,000 Sac order. My cousin, Tres, has the bright idea of opening our *own* store in the mall instead. We visit the various leasing agents for each center and face a similar dismal rejection by each one. We are embarrassed, dejected, frustrated, and desperate. We feel sad. Unable to keep the lights on, we've reluctantly begun trimming the business down to a skeleton crew as we fill leftover word-of-mouth orders from past customers.

At lunch one day, morbidly discussing what to do next, my phone rings. It's a number I don't know. I step outside. A brand-new mall called The Gateway is set to open concurrent with the Winter Olympics in downtown Salt Lake. They rejected our proposal a month ago but are now offering us a "temporary location" over the bridge in the heart of the center. We can "be there just through the holidays and the Olympics," but they will likely seek "a more appropriate tenant" after that. "Just don't make us look bad," they say.

A miracle. We'll take it. We don't skimp. Carpet, paint, neon sign, artwork, a big screen TV running movies on loop. We max out Tres's credit cards this time, because mine are still tapped from the factory build.

From day one, the Lovesac store is good vibes only, underscored by the thumping bass from our handcrafted mixtape CDs pulsating through its wide-open doors, come rain or shine. We invite everyone to just come in, flop down, and hang out. We're honestly just hoping people won't laugh at us, at first. Who even knows how to behave in a giant not-beanbag store in the middle of a swanky new mall? Much to our surprise, we clear six-figure sales in those few precious weeks before Christmas. Not only can we finally pay ourselves for the first time in Lovesac history, but after working open-to-close mall hours throughout the first month, we even get to hire a few others and begin to build out a team.

Game on.

"FROM DAY ONE, THE LOVESAC STORE IS GOOD VIBES ONLY, UNDERSCORED BY THE THUMPING BASS FROM OUR HANDCRAFTED MIXTAPE CDS PULSATING THROUGH ITS WIDE-OPEN DOORS, COME RAIN OR SHINE."

KEEP ONE HAND ON THE NOW AND ONE ON THE NEXT

While it is admirable to be willing to fix machines, fill Sacs, or sweep floors, we *must* find a way to somehow be all-in on the task at hand, *while* keeping the other hand on the next chapter as well … or face the consequences. Either a myopic focus on today's problems *or* a myopic focus on our imagined future, with no regard for reality, will lead us down dead-end roads. Sustained success can only come by juggling both. This is hard. If it were easy, everyone would do it.

The only way to escape *some* of the demands is to share the load: delegate, trust. Perhaps you subconsciously enjoy being a martyr—proving to everyone around that you're willing to work harder and go longer than they are, at any cost. You like to be the hero. I was like this. Perhaps you feel you can't spare the *time* to make that hire and train them up or afford the kind of talent that you need to level up. In reality, you can't afford *not* to. It is often when things are tight and most demanding that we must divert time, attention, and resources to finding the help we need and empowering others. But do not squander the resultant bandwidth gained. That extra time, energy, and headspace gained from delegation must be applied to "the next" or it is just an unnecessary expense.

This is what is meant by the commonly repeated idea of the need to be "working *on* the business, not just *in* the business." It applies to every person at any level, whether you are in a leadership role or not. We can work both *in* our job as we work *on* our job—developing our career, developing ourselves, developing those who work with us, and sometimes even developing our role itself to take on more, or become more useful to the organization. The bigger our ambition and the greater the potential opportunity is—the more time, energy, and investment we must focus working *on* it, not just *in* it. Always keeping one hand on the now and one on the next.

THE MOVE

March 2002. Still slinging Sacs all day at the mall, I've just witnessed an inquisitive customer inside pumping my cousin for information about "franchise opportunities."

Tres dryly gives them *my* card and tells them to "Call Shawn—he's the head guy."

"Of course, we franchise," I say, pressing the phone to my ear while escaping quickly through the open doors of our first location onto the bridge outside. "Which location have you seen? ... Oh, Salt Lake, that's a good one."

A month later, we not only have all the necessary agreements in order, but we have franchise deals lined up for Phoenix, Las Vegas, LA, and San Diego. Our first store is still cranking, and the mall is courting *us* now to sign a permanent lease. I somehow convince Scott, the attorney we've enlisted to get us franchise-ready, to leave his practice and join me as a partner, on a subsistence wage. We're going so fast, and I need next-level help. Scott is smart, grounded, and understands finance and contracts.

Tres and I pack up the truck with a few personal belongings and move to Huntington Beach, California, seeking a midpoint for all the stores we plan to open out West. Ulterior motive: Learn how to surf!

But before long I'm spending more time inside my *car*, stuck in I-405 traffic, than in all the California stores we've quickly sprung up between our company-owned locations and those of excitable franchisees looking to get in early. I'm doing interviews for store managers at local food courts during the day, then spending twelve hours on a ladder at night painting, hanging artwork, wiring speakers, installing lighting, and unloading trucks. We're also moving our Sac factory, tractor and all, from Salt Lake City to Tijuana, Mexico, at this time. I need to personally oversee this complicated process as well.

With most of my business partners, Dave, Scott, James, Christian, Chris, Jon, Dan, and Nate, still operating out of Salt Lake, running the books and back office, I make more than fifty drives between California and Utah just that year. Whenever possible, to be efficient in my travel, I pilot our one-ton Dodge truck towing a thirty-foot-long enclosed high-cube snowmobile trailer. It is loaded front to rear and top to bottom with shrunken, packaged Sacs fresh from our Mexico plant. I'm unloading it along the way, by hand, after mall hours, at each of our stores in neighboring states, now spilling over into New Mexico and Colorado.

Meanwhile, I'm building spreadsheets with detailed projections and specifications for millions of dollars' worth of China-made Sac covers and accessories necessary to support this exploding retail chain. I'm building these spreadsheets mostly by cut-and-paste with one hand as I drive through the night with my laptop balanced on the extra-large fold-down armrest of the eight-thousand-pound truck yanking the twelve-thousand-pound trailer in tow. I'll have to handle the accompanying bank wire in transit at whatever local Wells Fargo branch I'm nearest to in the morning, or we'll be out of key inventory in three months from now for our second critical holiday season.

Days matter. Hours matter. Minutes matter. I sleep when I can and where I can. I work in the seams and cracks. I burn through *weeks'* worth of minutes on the mobile phone each month, and thankfully—I survive. On one of these long drives, I arrive in Salt Lake just in time to appreciate a Lovesac Lounge setup by our guerilla marketing team at a huge party on the University of Utah campus. I am introduced by a friend to a beautiful, fierce, and talented girl named Tiffany.

I've dated plenty by now at age twenty-six ... but this one is different.

LESSON #11

WORK IN THE SEAMS AND CRACKS

Getting ahead is just hard. Really hard. It doesn't matter what job we're talking about. It doesn't matter how much money you're able to raise (always raise more than you think you'll ever possibly need). It doesn't matter how great your business partners or coworkers are (seek out the absolute best you can possibly afford). It's going to be hard no matter what, and if you want to get ahead, you'll need to be willing to give *everything*. It's not to say you can't juggle a relationship, play, sleep, nutrition, exercise, faith, family, hobbies, and all of that. But it won't be easy, and in the end, something always gives.

You must be realistic about that and cut yourself some slack somewhere—learn to live without perfection—even if you're a perfectionist at heart. The only way I've found to consistently keep up with most of it is to work (and play) in every seam and crack of life. There are minutes and hours and even days of our lives wasted inefficiently each week, in between, on the way to, just after, and sometimes even during the main events that populate our schedules. Drop and give me thirty push-ups in between video calls. Develop the muscle memory to dial up your loved ones as you walk out of a store visit, meeting, or business lunch—just to check in and say hello—just to keep things together.

Bluetooth your laptop or phone to your car or headphones in transit to take in the news, "read" a book, or audio-play PDF articles while in motion if necessary. Carry all the right gear: chargers, adapters, USBs, bank cards, log-ins, passwords, and documents with you most of the time so things can be accomplished from anywhere. Then, in the moments and events where you're face-to-face with real people (especially your partner or your kids) seek to be totally present. Make intentional eye contact, smile, enjoy yourself, and do your best to focus on *them,* even if only for a minute if that's all you've got. There *is* enough time in the day, week, and year to get *almost* everything done *and* enjoy the moment—but only if you're prepared.

And only if you develop the high-functioning habit of working in the seams and cracks.

THE MAYHEM

August 2003. Somehow between the store openings, staff trainings, franchise negotiations, and late-night deliveries, Tres and I make time, usually just before sunset, to park near the Huntington pier and paddle out into the ocean. We teach ourselves how to surf. We coordinate our first all-hands executive offsite at our rented beach condo in Rosarito, Mexico, that we've provided for Jon and his new wife. Jon is brave enough to relocate to Mexico and run the place as factory manager, after all. We all sleep on their floor, dish-soap-bubble-out the hot tub, launch M-80 rockets on the beach, surf, and repeat.

Our marketing team has us involved in every buzzworthy event possible by now. Not just another fashion brand, our Sacs can hold their own in celebrity venues at the Oscars, Emmys, X Games, and anywhere else people are meant to just chill. One friend leads to another, and suddenly all kinds of celebrities, musicians, athletes, and Hollywood superstars are reaching out to get their hands on one of these eight-foot-diameter "Lovesacs" everyone is buzzing about. The brand is really starting to boil. We may not know a lot about finance, planning, accounting, visual merchandising, or amortization of inbound freight, but we do know how to cause a ruckus. We offer 99 percent off to the first person in line at each new store opening and count down by 1 percent for every person in line thereafter. We're seeding the new market with our product, as marketing.

Fans are coming out and camping overnight, dressing up on-theme, and queuing up through the mall, stretching out into the parking lot. Our reputation precedes us for store openings. Our lines block the entrances of fifteen neighboring stores and generally piss off everyone along the way. Customers love it! We pay the Laker Girls to come out and take photos with our line of LA super-fans at our store opening in Redondo. We just have fun with it—with *all* of it. We make *work* our play.

We ride longboard skateboards in the parking lot at sunrise after a rough overnight build in Orange County where Jed will immediately take over as franchisee. We dip in the pool after a dawn surf session, doubling as a shower for the day. We wakeboard in the summer months behind friends' boats as we pass through Salt Lake for meetings. I squeeze in a paying gig as lead singer in my long-time cover band, at bars in Park City—making sure to pull a full trailer-load of Sacs through the desert en route. We play along the way. We date along the way. Thankfully, I get married along the way to Tiffany on August 13, 2003. After nearly five years going full speed nonstop, taking almost a week off for a honeymoon feels like an extravagant luxury.

Life is good.

PLAY ALONG THE WAY

"Play along the way" is perhaps my favorite Shawnism. Its roots tie back to a time when I was living in Taiwan for two years, as a nineteen-year-old volunteer missionary for the Church of Jesus Christ of Latter-Day Saints. As explained earlier, as a full-time missionary I had great ambition to become totally fluent in Mandarin. I'd memorize Chinese characters on flashcards even while pedaling my bike amid a sea of scooters. I'd practice and repeat phrases endlessly in all the seams and cracks before every meeting or appointment.

Once, we were all hanging out in the foyer of the church building killing time with some of the young Taiwanese locals our age, waiting for an appointment to arrive. This chipper girl named Candy was always the life of the party.

She eventually turned to me, and in a concerned voice asked, "Nelson ... are you alright?"

I looked up from my flash cards, busy memorizing more characters.

"Of course," I say flatly. "Why?"

"Because I never see you smile."

Whoa. What? Me? Nooooooooo. That can't be right!

This was one of those needle-off-the-record-moments for me. I was mister crazy—life of the party. Was I not? I was mister "everybody has a dream, love and care about every child of God, etcetera." Was I not?

Wait. What have I become?

I put down my flashcards sheepishly. Huge mistake. From that day forward I made a commitment to try to focus more on the *people* present than on the task at hand. Remembering, "Love matters." I realized that it is actually one of my superpowers to play like I do, hard and loud, and really *live* my life in real time, even *as* I work. This is *my* way to influence others for good ... perfect Chinese or not. I need to have more fun with it—even while riding a bike and wearing a suit and tie in ninety-degree tropical humidity talking religion and doing unpaid service projects. Ironically, this shift in behavior—to have more fun, live more in the moment, and focus on the people in front of me—made me an even more effective missionary in ways I can't describe. I continued to study my Chinese relentlessly--but only in the seams and cracks between, when people weren't around to engage with.

I returned home and traded in my sensible Toyota for the completely impractical red, roofless, resto-mod 1976 Ford Bronco that became my daily driver in college. Why? Because to drive it, even to run an errand, was *fun*. It was my loud, unmistakable calling card wherever I turned up in my twenties. I learned from this experience to *only buy things I love* and to *invest* in things that are *worth* it. We all have to make a car payment either way—you might as well really *love* the car you're stuck paying for, right? In my case, its V-8 engine also allowed for quick weekend jams to Lake Powell with four friends, one per seat, no-roof-no-doors towing my parents' second-hand 1982 Glastron ski-boat, 350 miles through the desert at night.

We'd enjoy the stars along the way, only to sleep out under them in the Lovesac tossed on the red sandy beach, once arrived. We'd wakeboard from dawn until dusk for two days and drive home too stiff to grip the steering wheel. Morning classes at the U, followed by Sac-stuffing and deliveries to the suburbs before waiting tables until midnight. All of this just so I could afford books, insurance, gas, dates, and the next trip to the lake during those precious college years, not knowing that Lovesac's meteoric growth would soon eat the next few decades of my life.

Take the time you need to keep yourself relaxed and sharp. Use up all of your paid time off if your job offers that. You're no good to anyone as a miserable, uptight, workaholic anyway. You won't perform well that way either. Work as hard as possible while cramming some good times into all the seams and cracks of life. You may have to make sacrifices along the way. You may have to skip *some* things and live without others for years. You may take shorter vacations or chase different kinds of hobbies than others do because of your ambitions.

To this day, in my forties, I've never taken a vacation longer than a week, but I *have* had plenty of fun along the way.

However you do it, push yourself to *play along the way* ... or twenty-five years will race by accidentally, and you'll just have gotten old.

"HOWEVER YOU DO IT, PUSH YOURSELF TO *PLAY ALONG THE WAY* ... OR TWENTY-FIVE YEARS WILL RACE BY ACCIDENTALLY, AND YOU'LL JUST HAVE GOTTEN OLD."

THE
MILLION

April 2004. I'm sitting on the bleachers in the parking lot of our Salt Lake store enjoying Lovesac VIP sponsor tickets to the Dew Tour national skateboard competition. I'm told these people holding clipboards down there want to speak with me. They're from a top reality TV production company out of LA. It turns out that Richard Branson, founder of Virgin (Records, Airlines, Megastores, Galactic), is spinning up a business competition reality TV show, and they want me to audition for it.

They're recruiting in most big cities across the country and heard of me by asking around at the University of Utah business school. It's for business-owner-entrepreneurs to compete for what will be the "biggest prize in reality TV history." But the specifics would remain a mystery to all of us until the last exciting episode.

We'll get to fly all over the world filming with Branson. I fill out their forms, shoot their on-camera interviews, and then forget all about it.

Three months later I receive a phone call: "Can you be ready to travel to London and begin filming next week? You'll need to leave your company behind for two months, and you'll have no contact with *anyone* during filming." No phones. No email.

I'm nervous. My business partners are nervous. My new wife is nervous. I'll have to miss our very first wedding anniversary, and if I get eliminated in an early episode, I'll apparently be sequestered to a hotel at an undisclosed location, where I'll have to wait alone for *weeks* with no contact, so as not to reveal the outcome of the show. But the exposure could be life-changing, not even knowing yet what the prize may be. Let's risk it! Push me out of the nest.

With each episode, we fly on Virgin Air to some crazy new destination: London, Hong Kong, Zimbabwe, South Africa, Japan, Morocco, Miami. We compete on teams doing business challenges. Then we do something crazy at each location, Richard Branson–style: like walk on a plank between hot air balloons at 10,000 feet over London, perform on stage in front of thousands at V Fest, leap from Victoria Falls in Africa, or practice space-walking in a zero-gravity plane for training astronauts.

Two months of filming, eleven episodes, and fourteen people eliminated, we finally end up on Richard's famous Necker Island in the Caribbean. It's down to me and Sara Blakely, founder of Spanx. She, of course, is amazing. Her business is further along than mine and Richard, being the generous benefactor that he is, makes a decision on the spot to sponsor a nonprofit as an extension of her mission to empower women, donating almost as much as the grand prize.

Then Richard turns to me and names me the winner. He gives me one last test for high drama. He presents to me a check for $1 million, a gift for me to invest in Lovesac. (Of course, we've already amassed $2 million in debt at this point, having grown so rapidly.) I can take this million dollars, or I can flip a coin. If I guess the coin toss correctly, we will "go on an even greater adventure together."

This is gut-wrenching. Each episode's challenge has come down to testing the contestant's capacity for either properly taking risks or *avoiding* outsized risks by showing good judgment. After thirty minutes of deliberation, all filmed in high-def on ten different TV cameras, I take the check for a million.

"There are just too many people who have given their lives and skipped paychecks when necessary to help me build this. I can't risk this windfall. This is life-changing money for Lovesac," I explain.

Richard laughs and reveals: that *had* I flipped the coin, he would have ruled me foolhardy, and I would have left the show with nothing! As part of the grand prize, I'm also named "President of Virgin Worldwide" for a few months. It's a cheeky title concocted for the show, but I would get to meet and work with many of the CEOs of his various Virgin brands for a season.

The cameras are finally put away after two solid months of filming every moment of every day. We're lying on the roof of the main house at Necker Island looking at the stars. It's just me, and Richard, and Tiffany, whom they flew down to surprise me, live on camera after I win, during the filming of this emotional final episode. The whole thing feels surreal. Our conversation under the night sky gets deep and philosophical. Richard asks me about my beliefs. I share my faith in God and my gratitude for blessings and miracles like this one. I ask about his.

Richard tells me, in that distinct English accent, "I believe we make our own luck."

I nod and smile. I'm not sure how I feel about assigning all the credit to luck. It feels dismissive to me at the time.

Oh well, just look at those stars.

MAKE YOUR OWN LUCK

The respect I have for luck would come still later in life, and you will see why. It's all too easy for the young and headstrong to correlate our successes with our own efforts, intelligence, charisma, and capabilities. The faithful choose to thank God as well. The undying optimist in all entrepreneurs will accept the inevitable rough patches as necessary stumbling blocks meant to be conquered.

But *really* tough times—the incredibly painful kind of hard times that stack up in layers and conspire with rotten timing to wreak havoc on our physical, mental, and financial viability—*these* experiences can cause us to finally capitulate and admit: *only terribly bad luck can possibly explain my plight.* Blaming God never feels right—faith or not.

After experiencing plenty of my own terrible luck in life, as you will see later, I have since come to believe very much that luck plays a role in *everything* ... but not in a dismissive way. My view, as a person of faith, is: God set this whole thing in motion, leaving room for random collisions and deflections as a feature, not a bug. Like asteroids in outer space colliding to form planets or butterflies affecting the weather.

Making an effort daily to openly express gratitude is one of the healthiest things we can do, whether you believe in God or not. In my case, through prayer. It keeps us humble and grounded. Even if we don't choose to look at things as "blessings," good luck is okay too. As I see it, even the ricochet of random events in this life are part of the cosmic landscape God expects us to navigate anyway. Because of this, life is *not* "fair," and it never will be. You just have to play it where it lies.

Speaking of luck … when we opened that first store way back in 2001, we hung the giant Lovesac neon sign out front with some anxiety, quietly knowing that we didn't own the national trademark for the name. We had registered the name "Lovesac" legally as a business in the State of Utah, but the moment we began to venture out of state, our attorneys forced us to come to grips with the fact that we didn't actually have trademark rights to license it out as a franchisor. The trademark, "Lovesac," had been registered since 1978 to a bedding company based in the Midwest. They didn't seem to be using it actively, but it had been renewed by them regularly for more than twenty years without interruption. No response to our calls.

In that short time span, as we negotiated through our first franchise agreements on the heels of that opening month at retail, the new year rolled over to 2002. Before we printed and sent the draft agreements that would by necessity disclose our need for an entirely new brand name, we checked USPTO.gov one last time on January 2. After more than *twenty years* of renewals, the registration had been abandoned. We snatched up the name "Lovesac" as a registered trademark for no more than the standard $250 application fee. Miracle.

Richard Branson was right, in the end. "We *do* make our own luck," or as they say, "Luck is where preparation meets opportunity."

By striving for excellence and developing various talents all my life, I had unknowingly prepared for a fast-paced trip to foreign lands with a billionaire—engaging in business competitions where speaking empathetically to foreign tribal leaders in Africa, doing daredevil stunts dangling from ropes off buildings, or singing Britney Spears songs onstage a cappella in front of ten thousand taunting Brits at a rock festival—that would somehow lead to victory. For my youth, I didn't choose to recognize it at the time. But certainly, winning "one million dollars on prime-time national TV," just in time to save my fledgling business from the debilitating debt we had already amassed, can *only* be attributed to some cocktail of good luck and blessings.

Call it faith. Call it "the secret." Call it a coincidence if you like. But we *do*, in fact, make our own luck.

THE SOFA

July 2005. Viewing each passing episode of *The Rebel Billionaire* back at home in Utah, as it airs live on prime-time network TV, is thrilling. With each weekly installment, we host an expanding number of people at our new Lovesac headquarters in the fashionably restored Salt Lake Hardware Building downtown. The crowd expected to view the final episode requires us to rent an entire concert venue, as thousands of Lovesac "friends" and family come out to watch the exciting conclusion on live TV together.

Tiffany and I, bound by contract, have had to keep the secret that I had won, for many months already. I now get to enjoy the unbelievable outcome on Necker Island all over again, this time with all my closest friends, family, coworkers, and media on stage to celebrate with me. What a relief it is to finally share the news. Catharsis. It's one of the best nights of my life, even as I'm served with a baseless unrelated lawsuit while standing on stage, just after winning, still bathed in all that confetti! Life in business—it never relents.

Now I'm off to London, New York, Sydney, Las Vegas, and LA! I'm slated to fly around the world again now, acting as "President of Virgin Worldwide," to meet with top executives from Richard's many Virgin companies. I'll give them my youthful take on their business models and road map, but I'll mostly learn from *them*. It's a dream. Venture capital groups are circling to invest in Lovesac as well. We're still not taken very seriously by the shopping malls, who see us as a beanbag fad, worthy only of the locations under the escalator.

But right from that first store, customers daily would ask us about the sofa in the corner, which was only there as part of the décor.

"How much is that?"

"It's not for sale."

"Yeah—but I like it—how much for the sofa?"

We can't deal with the sofa. It's too big to move and too heavy to ship. Stocking multiple sizes, shapes, fabrics, and colors is impossible for our little shops. If only we could shrink them down like we do with Sacs!

Recognizing the vast business opportunity in sofas, Dave and I dissect a dozen of them and work furiously on our own designs and prototypes that might allow us to break them down and reconnect them like LEGOs. No tools. Each piece is now separate, making it possible to fit tightly tailored covers that can be machine washable and changeable for endless combinations. We file for multiple novel patent claims on the mathematical formulas that make these "Sactionals'" geometry so useful.

We can't make the final prototypes ourselves. They require specialized equipment for the springs and upholstery. We take our samples to Joel, our first landlord—the sofa manufacturer who lent us that original shredder. We give him $1000 on contract to make us production samples based on our prototypes and drawings. We return in three weeks to see the samples, and he presents us with a traditional sectional sofa like the kind that has been around since the 1950s. Corner piece, middle piece, ottoman. It can be reconfigured a little, and it connects somewhat poorly. It's nothing new.

"Put these little sectionals in your mall stores, and they'll do great!" Joel says.

"Where is the *Sactionals* design we left you with, the Seats and the Sides?"

"Oh, that will never work. It won't be stable, it will come apart, it won't be comfortable, none of the angles are right. Trust me. I've been making furniture for forty years, and my daddy for forty years before that."

We're stunned—and frankly we're pissed off—that he didn't just do what we paid him to do. We take our homemade models and drawings next to Ed's custom upholstery. We've used Ed for other sewing projects over the years. We pay him $1,000 for a set of finished samples. We check back in three weeks to see our finished samples. Ed, as it turns out, does *the exact same thing as Joel*! He even *tells* us nearly the same thing.

I feel like I'm losing my mind. We think we're really onto something with this new design, but clearly the furniture experts don't agree.

Maybe we should just do it their way?

LESSON #14

MIND THE EXPERTS

People who want to build great things must surround themselves with as much expertise as they possibly can afford. Experts should be hired. Experts should be heeded. Experts should oversee their areas of expertise. In matters of design, for example, everyone thinks they have great taste and good ideas. But there are people who have trained for years to do it well. For the most part, I believe very passionately that you should always *let the designers do the designing.*

In dealing with experts of every kind, however, you must pay careful attention to the *one* voice that may need to override their expertise from time to time. You must listen to your instincts. You must trust your gut. It's a peculiar scientific fact that our brain stems have actual neurological connections that run directly to our gastrointestinal tract. It is unexplainable, and it can be difficult to describe, but we all have intuition. We all have gut instincts. Some more than others.

When you ignore your gut completely, in the name of complying with the "facts" as delivered by the experts, you are neglecting the ultimate difference-maker as a leader, and as a creator. *Your* instincts. Especially when considering something truly groundbreaking. The best ideas in any given field or industry rarely come from the experts inside of it. It is precisely their *knowledge* of that field that makes them *too smart* to truly challenge the same things that have already been challenged unsuccessfully before. They won't even try. It is *because* the furniture experts had made furniture the "right way" for so many years that they were simply not *dumb* enough to have created Sactionals the "wrong way," like we did.

Sactionals today have become, perhaps, the single best-selling couch solution in the United States—ever—and still growing. Joel and Ed are long out of the business. Expertise has its place. But Dave and I remained just *dumb* enough to look at these rectangles we had designed, and observe that because of their mathematical relationship with the geometry of the accompanying Side piece, they could be arranged and rearranged, deep-ways *or* long-ways, to achieve endless useful configurations. So why not? Looks cool to me. Let's try it. Let's go all the way with it and see if we can *make* it work. Let's push ourselves out of the nest and buy entire container loads, to see if we can't figure out how to sell them at scale.

Learn to mind the experts in their expertise. Defer to their know-how as much as possible. Most of the time they should be left to do their work and lead your organization to success. This is a good outcome for you. *Occasionally* though, when your gut really fights you, learn to mind them like you *mind the gap* exiting a train. Be wary, and occasionally be stubborn enough to fight for what you really believe in. Don't be afraid to stay a little bit stupid. And finally, be on the lookout for your own dream-crushing tendencies once you, after many years of experience and expanding knowledge, have become the expert yourself.

THE SACTIONAL

October 2005. Lovesac is a fun place to work. We're growing rapidly but still utilizing all of the concepts I learned as a "team-building and leadership consultant" years before while working in China. We have focused, even this early, on building a strong culture by *design*, not just by default. We identify the core values and principles we intend to live up to, from our scrappy startup mantra of "Make It Happen" to "Love Matters," a concept that is embedded in our very name. We pore over every detail of our office space and the vibe it conveys from conference room names that reinforce these values down to the music we play all day, every day.

We stand up a glass DJ booth where we take turns spinning during work hours and even into the night. It not only drives the energy in the office, but we stream it out *live* to our nearly fifty Lovesac locations across the nation! We can literally take live callers, requests, and make callouts to customers over the mic in real time, directly into every store, like a radio station. We're not interested in simply hiring people with the right qualifications, giving them a sufficient workplace and supplies to do their job, and then finding a way to squeeze it for profits alone. This is a chance to build more than an *office* for Lovesac. This is a chance to build the *culture* of Lovesac. Everyone who joins us has a dream … and if they're willing to spend some chunk of their life helping to build ours, *that* deserves respect—and a great place to work. We are connected. We are motivated. We are intentional. We are excited.

I'm just embarking on my fifth year of "front-line" store tours, where I'll spend most of November and December working in each Lovesac location, getting to know the people there and staying connected and grounded. I just sell alongside the team. I help customers. I do a bit of training and merchandising while I'm there—then I'm onto the next one. I will spend Black Fridays for the next *twenty years of my life* working and training in Lovesac stores, with the most important people *at* Lovesac—our front-line associates and our customers. The front line is where real learning happens in any organization. The front line *is* the brand as customers experience it.

With Sactionals now on their way, we see a future that is bright and big and vastly different from the traditional furniture brands we intend to compete with. We are absolutely exploding. But the cracks in our operations are also widening. Franchise store owners are frustrated with frequent product outages as we wrangle with high growth, poor funding, and haphazard planning. Employees are motivated and enjoying their time at work but are embarrassed to deal with angry customers complaining about out-of-stock lead times or quality.

"*Sactionals are here*" reads the giant in-store sign overhead. But how should a passerby even know what "Sactionals" *are*, yet alone take a multi-thousand-dollar risk on purchasing a couch from a not-beanbag brand they've only just heard of?

Our new VC investors are putting pressure on us to right the ship quickly, or else "they'll be forced to step in." Just when we appear to those on the outside like we're flying highest, expanding fastest, and involved with all of the hottest celebrities, events, and shows …

Lovesac is on the brink of collapse.

IT'S YOUR FAULT

This is a phrase we use almost daily at Lovesac still—but usually, not in the way you would think. Here is how I explain it to every new employee who joins our HQ team as they meet me during the onboarding process even today: I'm so glad you chose to join us. I think we've built a great culture at Lovesac, and I hope everyone can enjoy their experience here. But over time, if that culture falls off or goes sideways … if this becomes an uninspiring place to work that is no fun anymore … if it becomes negative and boring … if we perform poorly and Lovesac becomes riddled with politics and mistrust … it's your fault.

(Dramatic pause.)

You are part of it—you contributed to that. I will take the blame and feel the consequences for sure—it is my fault too of course.

(Dramatic pause, double dramatic pause.)

But if instead, Lovesac continues to grow, and thrive, and becomes an even better place to work, a collaborative and inclusive place where everyone is generally happy and enjoys each other's company while achieving top results ... it's your fault. *You* built that. You are part of it, and your daily interactions and behaviors contributed to it.

"It's your fault" simply means: own it. Own everything, good and bad. Don't allow yourself to blame others, even when others are to blame. Just own it. Take responsibility for everything you possibly can. Whenever something goes poorly, even when it involves the actions of others, first ask yourself:

What could *I* have done better? How could this be tied back to something *I* could have avoided or handled better or seen coming and reacted sooner? How did *my* actions influence this person (who may even be the obvious source of the "problem") to behave so poorly? Or how could *I* have put us in a position where this person wouldn't have been able to cause this problem in the first place, or influenced them positively toward a better result?

The tenuous state of Lovesac back in 2005 was *my* fault. I had not yet put into practice most of the lessons in this book. The resulting fallout became apparent. It would take me a few more years to connect these dots and, sadly, many stakeholders would pay the price for my own lack of experience, humility, and self-awareness at that time.

While my VC investors could have handled things differently as well, it was *me* who chose to work with them, and it was my fault that we weren't in a position to pursue other funding strategies or to generate cash flow more sustainably at that time. I had *some* experts onboard, but my sizable ego surely prevented them from being totally effective. I couldn't see around those corners at the time, but if only by virtue of my title, it was still my fault.

Successful, capable people *like* working with others who take responsibility. Successful, capable people can usually *see* who or what is actually to blame in a given situation or recognize the influence that some uncontrollable outside force may have had in a matter. They don't need to be told—they can see it. So, make sure you're on a bus with mostly successful and capable people. Excuses and scapegoats become unnecessary in such company. Then choose to outwardly accept responsibility for *everything you can*, always seeking to sincerely consider how *you* might improve going forward. Encourage transparent feedback from your team. The truth will always shine through.

This will raise your esteem in the eyes of the kind of people whose opinion you should *actually* care about anyway because most people just can't do this—even when something obviously *is* their fault. Make it *all* your fault. Apologize proactively and sincerely where necessary. Then brush it off, move past it, and commit to doing better next time. You will find support even through your mistakes if you truly own them.

Finally, when things go *right* and the accolades and rewards abound, there will be no need to say anything. There will be no need to self-aggrandize or take credit for all the exciting accomplishments anyway. You can deflect any praise, and put all the "blame" on others, giving *them* the credit, as you should. Because everybody who is anybody already knows:

It's your fault.

"CHOOSE TO OUTWARDLY ACCEPT RESPONSIBILITY FOR *EVERYTHING YOU CAN*, ALWAYS SEEKING TO SINCERELY CONSIDER HOW *YOU* MIGHT IMPROVE GOING FORWARD."

THE
BANKRUPTCY

January 2006. I'm standing outside of a four-thousand-seat auditorium in Oxnard, California, between sessions on some paid speaking gig where I'm expected to motivate would-be entrepreneurs and business owners to get bigger, better, faster. My phone rings. It's a call I've been dreading.

Our lead venture capital investor tells me, "The board is voting to file Chapter 11 tomorrow in Delaware."

My investors' point of view is: After a disappointing holiday season fraught with various operational issues, Lovesac clearly needs more growth capital and runway to reach profitability. Rather than reinvest, however, they could strategically file for Chapter 11 bankruptcy, and through the reorganization process, cancel our worst debts, purge our worst lease locations (the kind you have to sign up for to get the really good ones), dissolve the worst-performing franchise relationships, and buy back the best ones at fair market value to make them all company-owned stores afterward.

We would need to eliminate most of our HQ staff and hopefully repurchase the company out of Chapter 11 in about six months' time for less than it would cost them to reinvest now. Talk about humiliation. Exactly one year ago, I was on prime-time national TV as a hometown hero representing my state as the winner of the "biggest prize in reality show history." I was crowned "President of Virgin Worldwide" and viewed broadly as Branson's protégé.

Now, I have to walk back into this venue of cheering onlookers, to rile them up with my thrilling origin story and entrepreneurial epithets. I know full and well that by this time next week I'll be sitting in Delaware State Court, at a table across from opposing counsel, twice my age, who will be grilling me and drilling down into every contract and document this business has, to ensure there was no personal misconduct or malfeasance. But I put on a smile and deliver my speech to much applause. It's mortifying.

We'd be in Chapter 11 reorg mode for at least six months, wherein I would have to personally lead small teams of whomever doesn't quit, to many of the locations we had *just* opened. We have to do the messy work in the middle of the night after mall hours now shutting most of them down the same way we had just built them out, but faster. We'd have to fire-sale the inventory, dismantle the fixtures, saw cash-wrap counters in half to fit them into dumpsters, uninstall lighting and neon signs, and then quickly move on to the next one. Meanwhile, we're still open for business everywhere else! I'm expected to continue being an uplifting leader and keep the vibe alive at HQ and across the front lines amid all this carnage, and through each of the painful stages that would follow.

If we are to make it out the other side of Chapter 11, sales must stay strong so cash flow can support the business on just the remaining few store locations and website revenues. All of this swift action is taking place against the backdrop of bad press and embarrassing headlines, as those damaged by the fallout attack me and the company publicly. Customers can see much of this bad press and conflict happening as well, questioning whether our "lifetime warranty" would even mean anything with the company in such turmoil. This further hinders performance. I feel torn in a million directions. I am humiliated. But I compartmentalize. I show up for work smiling. I continue training and motivating in stores and at the office, and I even DJ live from time to time.

But I am physically, mentally, emotionally, and now financially destroyed.

QUIT OR KEEP GOING

The real reason I was in this predicament, ironically, is because I "just *did* the next thing" and charged off to California to open more stores haphazardly. This was a mistake. I didn't pause to consider that it might be the *wrong* next thing. Did we even know *why* that first store worked so well? Was it the mall? Was it the location within the mall? Was it the horizontal store layout? Was it the demography of the surrounding area? Was it our three years prior, building the Lovesac brand in Salt Lake City beforehand? Was it the fleeting effect of Christmas and the Olympics? Was it the name, the logo, the staff, the music—what was it?

I should have just taken the time to hire an extra staffer in that first store, stop selling, and take my hands *out* of the business. I should have stood in the corner, observed, and worked *on* the business—for as long as it might take to understand exactly *why* it was working so well—then turn *that* into a replicable playbook.

Had I known anything about finance, I might have done things very differently in those earliest days at retail. With just one or two very successful locations I could have easily raised plenty of growth equity from any number of reputable investors who roam this earth in search of smart concepts where they can grow their money. They *want* to give you their money if you have something scalable and reliable—you don't have to bootstrap it forever, scale it yourself on pure grit, or self-fund it with wanton franchise fees like we did.

Instead, at that time I knew none of this. My chosen partners knew little more. We charged off to just "make it happen," using brute force and determination. We modeled that classic business school blunder: grow too fast, go out of business.

The best part about dealing with the worst kind of outcomes, however, is that they greatly simplify your choices. As I dealt with the stress, workload, and emotions of everything related to reorganization, one day at a family dinner I reluctantly asked my parents what they thought. My parents had never really encouraged *or* discouraged me to pursue Lovesac. In fact, I think it always confused them. In those earliest days, it seemed like such a small-time endeavor for a kid with a full-ride academic scholarship, fluent in multiple languages, and several job offers waiting for him at graduation.

In fact, years earlier, I was sitting on the floor with a Sharpie on a string, drawing out a Supersac pattern when my mom walked by to retrieve something from the basement. She stopped and asked, in a carefully neutral tone, "Is this what you want to do?"

I looked up at her, silhouetted in the afternoon sunlight pouring into the high basement studio windows. I thought about it for a moment—really considered her question—paused, and then replied, "I just *feel* like I should keep going."

She smiled and walked on to get whatever it was she came down for.

That was then, this was now. It was dark, still winter, more than eight years since the founding of Lovesac and we're in the depths of this bankruptcy process. There were so many different people angry with me, out of their jobs, disappointed, ashamed, and suppliers financially harmed. Some were actively suing me. My parents had read all the ugly articles forwarded to them by "friends" being helpful.

I asked them: "What should I do?"

Even if we made it through this I'd be starting the company over with just a few stores, tight funding, and no friends. I'd have to earn my equity back somehow over time. Or I could just get out now and reinvent myself somewhere else to avoid further humiliation and the daily reminders of my failings. *What should I do?*

My mom thought about it for a while—really considered the question—paused, and then replied plainly, "You can either quit or keep going." She got up and left the room, probably not wanting me to see her getting emotional.

That's all there is when it comes down to it: quit or keep going. It is a choice, and that's *all* it is. It is a choice we all must make each and every day actually, regarding each and every endeavor. You either quit, or you keep going. Keep it simple.

I decided to keep going.

"THAT'S ALL THERE IS WHEN IT COMES DOWN TO IT: QUIT OR KEEP GOING. IT IS A CHOICE, AND THAT'S *ALL* IT IS."

THE RESTART

March 2007. We relocate the company out of Utah to a tiny office on the banks of a brackish canal in the low-rent industrial district of Stamford, Connecticut, just outside of New York City. Zero Utah-based Sac'rs make the permanent move with me at this time. I'm secretly a bit jealous to watch my founding partners scatter to find stable jobs in the wake of everything that has transpired. It has been a painful process for my *top* team who carry real legal and financial liability through all of this. Some are forced to pay a steep price. Some are forced into personal bankruptcy unable to settle the relentless lawsuits against each of the officers of the defunct organization. I feel tremendous guilt. It is now lonely and intimidating to rehire from scratch, overlapping critical positions for a few weeks as we manage this messy process across three time zones. *Just keep going.*

In Stamford, we can be closer to the oversight of our investors and gain access to everything New York has to offer. The million-dollar investment by Branson, along with my personal equity, is completely wiped out in the reorg. To add insult to injury, I'm expected to take a back seat inside my own company. A "workout guy" named Walt is brought in to help operate the business in the name of the creditors and investors through the Chapter 11 process.

I'M EXPECTED TO TAKE A BACK SEAT INSIDE MY OWN COMPANY.

I have no idea what my future holds, or any surety as to whether Lovesac can even survive on the short leash of capital we're allotted to build back on. I'm already working remotely from cheap hotels in Connecticut each week when I fly my young wife, Tiffany, out from Utah to "sell her" on the idea of making the move. We'd be leaving our extended families behind and moving to the East Coast for "two or three years" theoretically—just until Lovesac is big enough for us to find a financial exit.

As if on cue, a huge rat darts across her path as Tiffany is exiting the old Delta terminal at JFK airport as if to say, in its imaginary Queensboro accent, "Welcome to New York, lady." She shrieks into the phone as I'm waiting outside to welcome her for her first-ever visit to the area. I'm asking her to consider shuttering her own small business back in Salt Lake City, and leave everyone else she knows to move here with me for this unpredictable leg of our adventure. In deciding together to "keep going" with Lovesac, there is little room for debate. Lovesac is moving to Stamford, Connecticut, and so I am too. Thankfully, Tiffany is willing to "keep going" with me.

We sell most of our belongings and our beloved starter home in Utah only to choke on an East Coast–sized mortgage that barely affords us a compact New England townhouse. With one extra bedroom, we can hopefully start a family. I suck it up and *buy* the townhouse, out of the gate versus renting, because if I'm in, then I'm all-in with both feet. I need my investors and the few employees we have left to see that.

It's nearly impossible to hire at Fairfield County wages on a Utah budget. Lovesac has newly tightened purse strings held by its new cadre of turn-around investors. Tiffany is still remotely operating Pears, her own shoe boutique that she had opened back in Utah. She offers to fill in as logistics coordinator for us as well for a few months, just to help us through the tunnel. She'll answer to Doreen—a godsend of a local hire who, along with Ryan as our new CFO, brings the expertise and attitude to wear three or four hats each to help get us moving forward again. Tiffany is working in the office late one night, firing off emails and spreadsheets up to the night before she's ready to deliver our first child. Of course, we have no idea we're on the eve of the great financial meltdown of 2008–2009, which will bring us to our knees again, personally, and bring who-knows-what kind of upheaval to our recovering company.

We just can't seem to get a break.

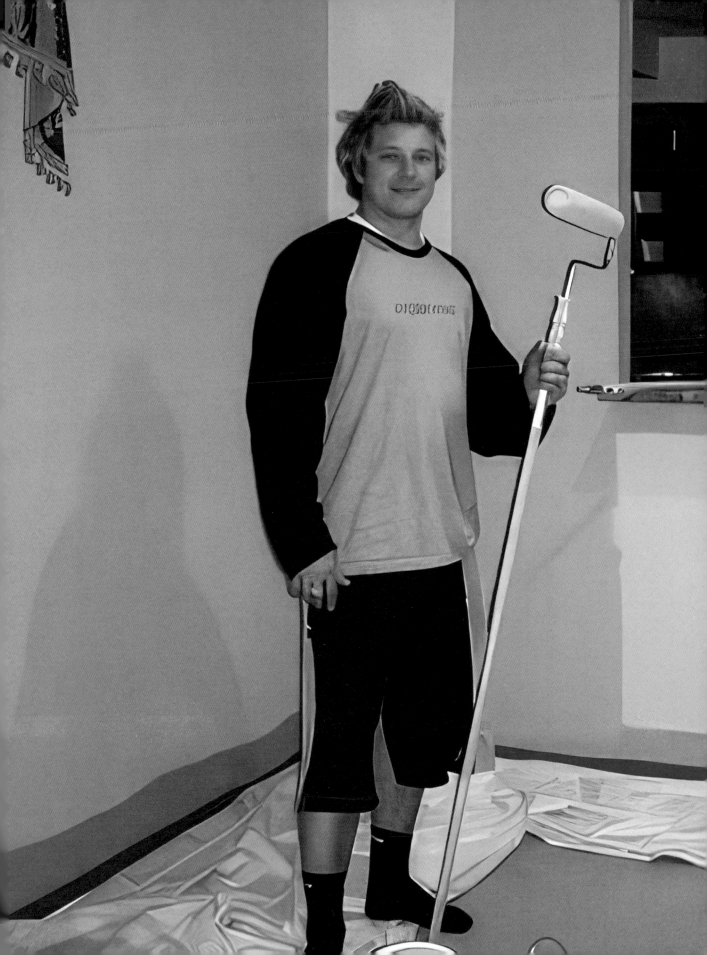

LESSON #17

EMBRACE UNCERTAINTY

There are many characteristics that entrepreneurs must exhibit to ultimately achieve great success. Grit, determination, work ethic, optimism, charisma, expertise, humility, et cetera. We've heard them all a thousand times and touched on many of them here already. But a rarely discussed ability that separates those who can survive it from those who will not is *the ability to thrive in uncertainty*.

Uncertainty, in its many forms, is by far one of the most difficult things for human beings to deal with in this life. Whether we recognize it or not, we are a comfort-seeking species who will subconsciously make decisions to avoid pain even over seeking pleasure.

One of the greatest sources of discomfort is uncertainty. We will make counterproductive decisions just to remove it from our life.

Uncertainty is oppressive. It lingers and looms over us as we try to sleep. It hijacks our thoughts from the moment we wake up. It may be as transient as the time it takes to hear back about the outcome of a test or application. It may be as enduring as a decades-long pursuit that threatens *never* to work out in our favor. It may be a threat that can ruin us financially or reputationally should it take a wrong turn. It may be in the form of the unpredictable behavior exhibited by others whom we wish we could depend on.

Uncertainty may take on the form of having to give up ownership control to raise enough money to afford the growth capital and talent you need. Raise the money. Or, if you're not the owner, take the job and work your way up. Control by ownership is an illusion. Be *good* enough to allow your work ethic and performance to speak for itself under the harsh light of measured results.

Who controlled the 1990s Chicago Bulls? The coach? The billionaire owner? Michael Jordan did ... because he was the best.

Just be the best. Regardless of your current position, or what the cap table says, and regardless of the ownership dynamics, your board of directors' oversight, or the disposition of your "boss." If you're willing to be the best, you can play in the big leagues without worry. This requires self-awareness, confidence, and integrity on your part, along with truly good investors, partners, and team members as well. Choose wisely. But most of all, just be *awesome*! Do that, and you have nothing to fear.

Whatever the case, the ability to accept, push forward, and even *thrive* in uncertainty is the difference-maker when it comes to great ambition. Learn to recognize uncertainty for what it is. Learn to just roll with it—like getting rolled over by a stray wave in the ocean, knowing you'll eventually come up for air. Stay relaxed as you spin, lest you panic and make it worse. Focus only on the things you can control. Just roll with the rest—let it go—ignore it. Learn to focus on the people or the task at hand despite uncertainty's ever-present cruelty. Learn to enjoy the life happening to you *right now*, even as ambiguity attempts to weigh you down. Compartmentalize. The ability to be flexible and thrive in any kind of uncertainty is the elusive quality that true entrepreneurs share.

But entrepreneurship is overhyped anyway. Entrepreneurs are overrated and overcelebrated in our culture. Not everyone *should* aspire to be an entrepreneur.

Where would the world be without doctors, nurses, electricians, engineers, teachers, construction workers, city planners, full-time moms, or employees of every kind? There are a million ways to make a buck, and entrepreneurship is just another one. It can pay well, but it comes at a cost.

Where would Lovesac be without the thousands, already, who have chipped in and spent a piece of their life here building it together? To be honest, just choosing to *join* an ambitious company like Lovesac is an entrepreneurial endeavor that should be recognized and celebrated. That said, *learn to embrace uncertainty* if you have ambition. It will serve you well.

"THE ABILITY TO ACCEPT, PUSH FORWARD, AND EVEN *THRIVE* IN UNCERTAINTY IS THE DIFFERENCE-MAKER WHEN IT COMES TO GREAT AMBITION."

THE BUS

June 2010. Our "three-year plan" that I sold Tiffany on when moving out to Connecticut has quickly come and gone, but thankfully Lovesac is still alive and kicking. Tiffany is literally lying on the hospital bed, recovering from the birth of our second child, signing short-sale documents on the tiny townhouse we're now upside down on after the unforgiving financial crisis reset. Huge loss. Back to renting. No tangible assets. But we need more space and a yard for our now-toddler-daughter, Lucky, and newborn son, Duke. Our credit scores will have to pay the price.

Thankfully, my clever new partner, Nancy, and I take advantage of the situation to negotiate for new and better lease rates within the top shopping malls across the United States, after the failure of so many retail brands throughout the financial crisis. Lots of great real estate is opening up. We're able to secure funding to do so from an unconventionally brave private equity group called Mistral, out of NYC, led by Andy Heyer who stumbles across us in the mall and takes an interest.

It's time to be bold again. We're unable to afford the PR teams and product-placement budgets we blew through in our first come-up, but we can pretend. We buy an old RV and have it wrapped calling it "The Lovesac Bus." I'll drive it myself when necessary and use it to network to partner-ships again with celebrities, upcoming pop stars needing a tour bus, and high-profile events like the Sundance Film Festival and the X Games. Each winter, I cross the country in it, still working and training personally, in each location over the holidays.

I've always been brashly vocal in plenty of interviews and articles, pro-claiming that "someday there will be Lovesac Theaters, Lovesac Buses, Lovesac Limos, and Lovesac Hotels ... on our way to building a lifestyle brand."

Marc Cuban gets wind of all my big talk and calls me up to give us a shot at reviving one of his more dated movie theater locations on "Lover's Lane" in Dallas. We'll be outfitting it with Sactionals and Sacs, front to back. I design the theater myself and make the ask at a time when we really need a big sale like this to bridge us to the funding from Mistral, lest we end up insolvent *again* as the due diligence investment process drags on. Six months later, I spend a week straight on my hands and knees, personally installing angled Sactionals' feet and "shoes" to mitigate the slant of the old auditorium's sloped floor. My handyman cousin Eric is enlisted to help me out. The Lovesac Theater at The Inwood quickly becomes the most popular auditorium in town. It's a big sale for us at a most critical moment. Miracle.

Meanwhile, our own Lovesac stores need a facelift in order to escape the retro college-kid vibe we were founded on and to become a legitimate furniture brand worthy of Sactionals' five- or ten-thousand-dollar price tags. But we have tight budgets—keeping the business incredibly lean until we have enough scale to begin generating cash from operations.

I practically live on a ladder once again with Eric, after mall hours, for two straight years alongside Justin, our new head of store design, who I've successfully poached from the architectural design firm we used for our latest rebrand. We steal Torin from his front-line sales job and live on the road together--upgrading every store location we can make it to. Fingers cracked from installing wall fixtures, frames, shelving, and lighting by hand as we run on zero sleep. Chafed. Famished. Just turn up the music louder and power through the night.

We're installing new artwork, rewiring sound systems, spray-painting makeshift cash-wrap-expansion legs in the parking lot—one location at a time. We become familiar with every aisle and bin location at Home Depot across dozens of cities. We're living out of a suitcase, sharing rooms, and going two or three days straight without sleep. This is followed by early morning training sessions for the managers and staff on improving their customer demos, and how to better utilize the new store layout we leave them with. Then it's on to the next one, with countless more needing similar upgrades.

I'm only thirty-three, but I'm exhausted.

The Mobile
LoveSac®
LOUNGE

The Lovesac Bus has been
Pimped By ChiefSac, Shawny D.

Sacs in mirror are
as large as they appear

If this bus is a-rockin' don't knock harder.

OVERSIZED SACS

LOVESAC

If you can read this, go faster.

lovesac.com is not a dirty web site

119·404

TALK BIG, WORK SMALL

Paint the picture. Any leader should be constantly talking big and "painting the picture" with words, pictures, presentations, and conversations to bring people along with their vision. It's too easy for employees, partners, investors, and suppliers to lose sight of the vision you are working toward, if it is not constantly reinforced. This affects their commitment as well as their ability to contribute fully, not for lack of desire, but it's easy to get lost in the forest for the trees when working in the details down at tree-level.

Tell your team what to expect, and what is coming. Get out ahead of everything you can and eliminate surprises wherever possible. Overshare. Set internal goals high but try to keep external expectations low. Beat them reliably. It is the leader's job to speak with boldness and transparency, including some of the bad news too. Keep it real. Be honest and candid. Don't sugarcoat everything—this weakens believability overall.

Share as much information as you appropriately can, and don't hoard it. Locking others out from vital information or key contacts is a feckless way to preserve control. Empower your team by keeping them in the know wherever you can. There are always things that must remain confidential, so be extremely disciplined with those, careful to not play favorites or betray trust.

Learn to communicate well, practice if necessary, and then overcommunicate the vision and values that shape the overall strategy. You must be thoughtful and careful with language, the naming of projects, products, and programs to reinforce key concepts through repetition and tradition. Tradition breeds coalition, and traditions gain strength with age—so plant the seed. As they say: "The best time to plant an oak tree was 20 years ago, the second best time is *now*."

Be consistent with your language and relentless on weaving the biggest ideas into conversations that tie back to your stated purpose, mission, and guiding principles on repeat. Do not relent—repetition is necessary. Then do as you say. Nothing destroys a culture like hypocrisy, empty platitudes, or unreachable targets. Where you come up short, call it out publicly, own it, regroup, and recommit. Never lose sight of the big picture.

Don't be shy about sharing the big picture with everyone you can. Share your biggest and most ridiculous ideas too sometimes, whether literal or just illustrative of your ambitions. This is a great way to "try things on." See how people react. See what grabs their attention. Or see what is just patently absurd.

You can try things on verbally to vet which concepts might have some merit. Say them out loud and describe them in some detail. Just see how they *feel* as you share them and pay careful attention to how others react. Some may resonate and take on a life of their own, like the Lovesac Limo did after some *other* entrepreneur heard me describing what it could be, half-jokingly, just for fun in an interview. Same with the Lovesac Theater example. Both really happened—conjured up by a passing comment.

Meanwhile, as the saying goes: "Don't believe your own press." There are all sorts of grand things we might say to get attention. There are all sorts of grand things others might say *about* us to make a headline read better or to embellish the otherwise innocuous truth.

As good as it feels to hear praise and be celebrated, *you* know the truth behind the scenes, and it usually isn't glamorous. Don't forget that. Stay grounded. Have the grit to turn around and focus on the drudgery of just moving the work forward day by day.

Get to know people at *all* levels of your organization, whatever your position is. Seek out mentors and be humble enough to learn from everyone. Be customer-centric. Speak to individual customers. Listen to them. Many of the best answers and ideas are found there—but you need to be in touch.

Find ways to get in touch and stay connected. Be willing to reply to emails and DMs. Be willing to meet deadlines and achieve your basic KPIs and goals with operational excellence. Even majestic visions, ideas, and plans can't excuse the baseline requirement to deliver solid performance week after week at your core "job," whatever that is (and we all have one).

Talk big, even as you work small.

"OVERCOMMUNICATE THE VISION AND VALUES THAT SHAPE THE OVERALL STRATEGY. YOU MUST BE THOUGHTFUL AND CAREFUL WITH LANGUAGE."

THE GRIND

July 2014. We're hosting our fourth annual "ManagerFest" in the backyard of my current business partner, Nancy, not far from our Connecticut headquarters. Tradition is powerful, and ManagerFest has quickly become a highly anticipated piece of our culture-crafting efforts over the years. In the most obvious way, Lovesac's culture has always been a reflection of its name and namesake product. Laid-back, fun, disarming, down-to-earth, gregarious LOVE ... and big, loud, bold, oversized SAC. Through thick and thin we've always maintained our biggest ambitions, hopes, dreams, and goals, even while hanging onto our willing-to-sweep-floors, make-it-happen, hard-working, fun-loving, startup kind of culture.

We want everyone to be an owner so we endow each of our fifty or so store managers and numerous HQ staff who have joined over the past year with some stock in the company. This gifting of stock in the company is a highlight of "ManagerFest," the most infamous week of meetings we have each year, and a tradition that would continue indefinitely.

My phone rings—it's my wife, she's breathless. The baby is coming, and it's time to go to the hospital. I wrap up my speech immediately by shouting in typical fashion.

"Who is Lovesac?"

The veterans in the group understand the assignment and reply in unison, "We are."

"Who is Lovesac?"

Louder, "We are!"

I'm now walking on top of the white linen tables, leaping one to the next, accidentally knocking over a few glasses, and shouting wildly, "Who—is—Lovesac?"

"We aaaaaare!!" The entire #LovesacFamily is standing and laughing with me as I hop off the table at the far end and just keep running for the gate out to the driveway, explaining over my shoulder, "I gotta go! Heading to the hospital. Number four is on the way!"

Time on the chair in the corner of the delivery room playing catch-up while waiting for closer contractions feels like a luxury. I'm buried in emails for work, articles for school, and church class preparations. Following my own instincts to level up, I'm currently enrolled to pursue a master's degree at Parsons, in New York City.

Meanwhile, I'm asked to be a volunteer youth seminary teacher for my church—waking up at 4:30 a.m. daily to prepare and deliver courses on ancient scripture to cheerful teenagers at 6:00 a.m., before they head off to high school each weekday. Grow Lovesac in the day. Ride the train into Manhattan each afternoon, cramming in all the required readings while in transit, just to keep up with the demands of a master's program at the world-famous Parsons, The New School for Design.

I'm exhausted but trying hard to be present. Tiffany is a gold-medal-worthy mom and somehow able to keep it all together for us as I do my best to *enjoy the grind*, every day, careful not to wish it away. These precious years with toddlers are demanding to no end, but we both recognize we'll never get them back.

Little Valentine is born early in the morning on the following day. She is doted on by her still-in-diapers, two-year-old sister, Pepper, along with Duke and Lucky too. This forces at least a few days' break for all of us—a break to be with Tiffany and *all* of my kids now, and just enjoy the moment.

As proud as I am of the company and the culture we're rebuilding at Lovesac, these are the moments and the people who matter most. Everything else is dust.

EVERYTHING ELSE IS DUST

One time in the 1990s, when I was fourteen, my parents took me and a friend on one of our many family trips to Lake Powell for a few days. It's my favorite place on earth. Our trips were never fancy—we just camped at the shoreline near the boat ramp, living out of our 1979 tan-and-rust-colored Dodge van. We would swim and waterski, wakeboard, and tube behind our little motorboat from dawn until dusk. Bonfires at night.

On the way home, thirty miles up the road after leaving the lake, my dad checked the mirror and noticed that his aftermarket locking gas cap was missing. He proudly outfitted the van with it just a few months before to keep those "damn kids" in the neighborhood from potentially stealing the gas out of our tank. He pulled over to inspect.

I knew what would come next.

My dad summoned me outside. "Shawn. Shawn!" Barefoot on the scalding pavement I hopped to the back of the van, shuffling to balance on the white painted line, which was tolerable.

"Where is the gas cap?"

"Um ... I must have left it on the bumper after emptying the gas cans into the van like you asked," I said uneasily.

He proceeded to berate me for a minute or two citing my stupidity and ungrateful attitude toward our family's things, and things in general.

"Why don't you think? Why don't you *think*!" He shouted several times as he stomped back to the driver's seat slamming the door. It was obviously loud enough so my friend inside couldn't pretend to have not heard it when I returned to the back seat in awkward silence for the long ride home.

My dad was generally a nice guy, and he taught me many things about many things. Camping, hiking, fishing, maintenance, construction, repairs, carpet, sheetrock, painting, woodwork, plumbing, electrical, cars, boats, engines, radios, real estate, hard work ... and how to make people feel less important than *things*. I vowed I would never do that.

To this day, I push *myself* to share anything I own with whoever asks, summoning the attitude up front: "Even if it gets destroyed, I will be cool and kind and express concern for *them*, without imposing guilt—not even subtly."

I'm still trying. *Things* are great. I enjoy lots of *things*. The right things can be tons of fun and make life exciting. But people must come first, or the things must go.

People are three-dimensional. *Everyone* should be respected, loved, and appreciated for the human beings they are both inside and outside of work. Everyone needs hobbies. Everyone is chasing different goals. Everyone needs time off. As I established in the introduction to this book: *everybody* has a dream ... and it usually has little to do with their "job." Even high-performance cultures must allow room for people to *live*—punctuated by necessary periods of demanding commitment.

Every company, large or small, is a company of *people*, just like a family of people ... a collection of flawed individuals, each on their own journey, but stuck together and expected to get along. Roles differ. Titles differ. Compensation differs.

But as *people*, each of us has equal importance. Build a transparent culture where love and respect abound. Seek out *good* people. Good, honest people strive hard naturally to achieve their professional goals, which can be measured in money, numbers, growth, or position, even in demanding times. Without good results our income and our collective well-being is threatened. But we can simultaneously prioritize how we *treat* people along the way. It's difficult. It's imperfect. But that is the challenge.

Things come and go. There is nothing wrong with aspiring to own things, collect things, and enjoy things ... especially more sustain-able things. Personal aspirations and even material ambition help drive us, *and* drive our teams forward. But the things don't *matter*. Principles matter. People matter. *You* matter.

Everything else is dust.

"PRINCIPLES MATTER.
PEOPLE MATTER.
YOU MATTER."

THE SHOWROOM

August 2015. Having finally scraped our way back to more than fifty locations, it has become apparent to me and to my investors that it's time for a change in direction. I owe a lot to the couple of turnaround partners who helped bring Lovesac back from the brink. I am grateful. But our strategy has drifted, and I can now see a better path.

We've gone too far into furniture-land. We're selling rugs, bowls, baskets, light fixtures, credenzas, and decorative accessories supported by ever-changing seasonal, themed lines. This is how the rest of the industry does things. We too are not immune to the waste, inefficiency, and complexity that comes along with this traditional retail model. I can see the emerging digital-first and direct-to-consumer brands out there that are focused on an e-commerce-led strategy, supported by small-format mall stores just like ours, but driven by advertising.

We're fifty locations ahead of most of them, and we have strong operational bones having built it up the hard way, versus the raise-tons-of-cash to burn-tons-of-cash business model that is confoundingly popular at this time. Our washable, changeable, rearrangeable, guaranteed-for-life Sactional is the obvious candidate to dominate the massive couch category. We need to get narrower, not broader. Focus.

We've never spent any *real* money on advertising to date, and to do so, I will need the right partner. After nine years with my head down swimming, doing whatever was necessary to push things along and rebuild using the furniture retailer strategy, I seek out a fitting "number two" for this new era. I need a true *partner* to serve as my president and COO, with the right credentials to carry us into this next chapter at Lovesac. I can see it will require a complete redesign of our branding and stores.

I *must* get this right. Another reset now would spell the end. I know if I can get this *one* decision right, so many other things will fall into place. I can feel the gravity of this pivot even as it's unfolding. After a long recruiting process, I choose Jack Krause—a brilliant business leader with a strong background in both specialty retail and classic CPG, consumer-packaged goods brand marketing.

Honestly, it has taken me nine years in partial exile, four kids, a master's degree, and a lot of growing up to achieve the maturity and humility to know how to recognize and empower real talent like Jack. With his leadership and expertise, we engage in all the right consumer research and listen to our *customers* to reveal what the future can look like. It requires us to peel back the onion and dismantle much of the past nine years of effort toward becoming a credible "furniture" brand in the traditional way. We'd make Sactionals the star of the show and jettison 80 percent of the other home décor products we have expanded into over this last decade. Do less and do best.

We take a risk first on local, then regional, then national TV advertising, supported by digital and social media, focused intently on measurable return-on-ad-spend (ROAS). The numbers don't lie. We leverage world-class branding and design firms to reimagine everything from our logo to our colors, and our showrooms to our product names. We test them all against customer feedback.

From here on out, we won't even operate "stores" anymore, with their endless seasonal changeovers, operational waste, and product-stocking inefficiencies. We will focus on forever-products, converting our stores into "showrooms," a place to touch, feel, and experience our amazing inventions that you might have seen on TV, online, or on your mobile device. These showrooms are reimagined with the new logo and teal branding. They will carry no inventory. Customers can make their purchase however they want, virtually or in-person. Everything will be shipped to them direct-to-consumer regardless of where they purchase.

It works.

HIRE BETTER THAN YOU, AND LET THEM OWN IT

Leaders end up getting the credit, whether they seek it or not.

"Steve Jobs created Apple, Pixar, and the iPhone."

But did he? Brands and products *that* complex are undoubtedly the work of many people across many teams. This is obvious. But Jobs gets the credit nonetheless.

Early in my career, even though I often hired older and more experienced people, placing them in top positions—if I'm honest, I found my own ways to undermine their work by needing to be personally involved in *everything*. Whether this was driven by my own ego or by the false notion that others need to *see* me driving things to be taken seriously as a leader, I am not sure. I certainly wanted all the "credit." But that approach failed.

Top talent and top teams, operating without too much dysfunction, deliver top results. End of story.

It is always in any leader's benefit, therefore, to hire the absolute best people they can possibly afford—and campaign to afford even better ones at that. The more threatening, on paper, top talent is to the leader's own job, the better. While in reality, they're *no* threat because the best people *are* extremely ambitious but maintain a low ego and are not cutthroat personalities, of course.

Be brave enough to hire people that are *even better than you*—at least in some capacity, if not overall. If you *yourself* are good enough, and you have helped build a culture that is conscious, loving, respectful, loyal, and enlightened enough, then there is no real threat to you anyway.

Over time I have been inside of and exposed to teams and organizations of every size, across many industries. They're all totally screwed up. Get used to it. Never let the glaring deficiencies of your organization bring you down. Just level up your team relentlessly. Fight the entropy. Allow first dibs to those that joined early, who have the capacity to adapt and grow. Be as loyal as possible—but ultimately, make the outcome for the *total* group your top priority. You owe it to them. Many lives are at stake. A-players attract more A-players. They are repelled by cultures that tolerate ineptitude.

The quality of your team is *the* source for the executional excellence you aspire to. Even so, the biggest of the big organizations still wrestle with politics, infighting, disagreements, and misalignments. You will climb this ever-eroding sand hill forever and battle it with hires, fires, and intentional culture sculpting—that is the job.

So choose people you *like*, at least, people you *can* like well enough. You're doomed to spend a lot of time together. But avoid hiring friends. Work from the top-down. Get it right at the top and the rest has a way of taking care of itself. Get it wrong at the top and it may take two years just to find out, and then two more to recover. Do not be casual about your top team—and be brutally honest with yourself and with them.

Hiring top talent is *still* not enough. You must also be courageous enough to let them hold the reins. Trust them. Let them call the shots. It took me a long time to learn that even though some leaders might do things very differently than I would in their situation, that doesn't make "their way" *wrong*. Who's to say that my way was *right*? As long as the results are good, and in line with the overall strategy you've set, then learn to let most things go. Pride of authorship has no real value.

Let them make *every decision you possibly can.* Let them own it. Even let poor decisions (if relatively harmless) play out from time to time so they can learn hard lessons for themselves. Finally, let *them* take the credit for success. There is plenty of credit to go around.

We must always balance the development of people with the pursuit of results. It is an imperfect art, not a science, and it is difficult—but that is the burden of true leadership. The irony is, with great results will come great praise. And while the conscious leader will deflect *all* credit outwardly to their team, that leader will *still* get the lion's share of credit anyway—probably an undue amount. That's just the way it works. So give it all away whenever you can.

Learn to swap "I" for "we," using "we did x" or "we thought of y" whenever possible, even if it *was* you. Make "we" your default language. Make it a habit. Top talent may go on to achieve positions or titles to the side, above, or beyond that leader who initially brought them on. This too reflects most favorably on the leader who hired them or coached them up. Be that person.

Hire *better* than you, and let them own it.

"WE MUST ALWAYS BALANCE THE DEVELOPMENT OF PEOPLE WITH THE PURSUIT OF RESULTS."

THE PHILOSOPHY

January 2016. Only four months after joining me at Lovesac, Jack and I are in the middle of yet another classic bullheaded Shawn-battle. I've always been adamant that my strongest instincts are usually right, and while I'm not always great at communicating *why* I believe in something, I *do* intuitively know "right" when I see it.

This kind of "founder's gut" should not be ignored. But it can be very hard to deal with in the context of a disciplined and professionally managed organization with ambitions to scale.

Jack, always patient with me, then challenges me in a way I'll never forget.

"What is your founder's philosophy?" he asks, with a defiant gaze.

"What is the unique design philosophy that separates *this* brand from all the rest? If you can articulate that, then the answers to so many tactical arguments like this one we're having right now, become obvious and easy to resolve for everyone in the organization."

His question washes over me like a tidal wave. I get quiet. I can't believe I'm unable to answer that clearly after all these years pushing Lovesac forward. I leave the meeting deep in thought. I spend the next few weeks unable to concentrate on anything else.

I spend months searching for the answer. I study our customer research, run tests, poll our employees, and pore over our social media and that of our competitors for clues. I've completed my master's degree from Parsons School of Design and have been asked to stay on as an instructor. I am steeped in the language of design thinking, sustainable business models, leadership, and innovation. So much of the reading I was exposed to as a student, and now prepare lectures on, as an instructor, contributes to what will become the most valuable insight for Lovesac that ever will be, all thanks to Jack's insightful challenge.

We call it: Designed For Life (DFL).

DFL is a concept that will shape our future, our culture, our products, and our Lovesac brand forever. DFL, put simply, means everything we design must be built to last a lifetime and designed to evolve as life changes. DFL ensures our originality in the marketplace. It is ownable. It is a totally unique approach to product design and branding. DFL demands that we design evolutionary *platforms*, not just products.

This is rare. It leads us to a stated "higher purpose" that is also unique and a little bit controversial: "We will inspire humankind to buy better, so they can buy less."

If we are right, and our products resonate with people because of these attributes, and thus sell extremely well, there will ultimately be fewer couches (and other things) sold on Planet Earth—because DFL things can actually *sustain*.

A strategy that ultimately results in people buying less stuff is a strange pursuit for a company that sells *stuff*. In fact, this "shrink the pie" mentality goes directly against the entire academic body of literature and theories on modern marketing, which all advocate "growing the pie" as a fundamental approach to drive scale.

But pies have grown too large. All product categories have been inflated, like a tumor grown out of control, fueled by cheap overseas labor, on the backs of unwitting consumers being conned into thinking their pants are too loose, too tight, too long, then too short—along with myriad forms of planned obsolescence, built into *everything we buy*. But we at Lovesac find this to be an extremely motivating purpose to live up to. We are the antithesis of planned obsolescence. We are happy to go directly against the grain to pursue *true* sustainability, accepting of the consequences.

The implications are many. For us to grow leveraging this counterintuitive philosophy, we will be forced to innovate successfully into other product categories to achieve sustained growth. We can't just sell the consumer the same product over and over again, like many of the biggest companies in the world do because our products *sustain*. We want them to sustain.

We will also pursue sustainable and circular operations on principle. Circular Operations (CO) will include services that unlock DFL products' real value. We won't just sell you a modular couch (or other things yet to come), we'll help you upgrade it, maintain it, add to it, re-cover it, trade-in used pieces to others who can utilize them after you can't, or help you completely redecorate. Given enough time, all of the products and all of these services are coming--in pursuit of true sustain-ability. This takes investment. We accept this. But with this clear design philosophy to approach new categories, and a higher purpose driving us, we are up to the task.

We aim to shrink *all* the pies eventually. This bit of gold, this key philosophy, only materialized because I was finally prepared to receive it. Because I have the right caliber of people around me to draw it out, to help connect the dots, and to execute on it as well.

Lovesac *is* Designed For Life.

Built to last

These <u>2</u> patented pieces enable you to create any arrangement you desire. You can rearrange it and even add to it forever because each piece is guaranteed for life.

How it all connect

Our patented locking system requires no to Shoes and Clamps secure Seats and Sides from above and beneath—creating one connected couch, even more durable tha typical static sofas. Included with each Se and each Side is one Shoe, one Clamp, and removable Feet—more than enough to build any configuration possible.

Clamp

Designed for life

Aside from being built to last, if a product can't adapt with us and our ever-evolving lives, then it falls short. This is true sustainability.

Truly great products *are* beautiful, making the life of the user easier and less stressful. You don't just buy a designed-for-life product. You invest in it.

We build products for life. For real life. For your whole life.

Shawn Nelson
Founder

KNOW YOURSELF AND KNOW YOUR PURPOSE

Back in 2002, as we expanded all across the West, we were already hiring dozens of people. I read a life-changing book early on called *Emotional Intelligence* by Daniel Goleman. He coined the term "emotional intelligence," and it has since become widely used in various professional circles. Goleman argues: the key to developing emotional intelligence is rooted fundamentally in self-awareness. This book was formative, and thankfully I discovered it early in my career. Whenever I am interviewed and have been asked that timeless question over the past twenty-five years, I've responded the same way: *The* secret to success is self-awareness.

Self-awareness is the source from which all other positive attributes and strengths can grow. It enables empathy—the ability to decipher and understand how *others* feel. These two abilities are the foundation for leadership and learning. Understanding who we are. Understanding people. Understanding customers and what they want—it all begins by first seeking to know yourself.

Seek. Observe. Contemplate. Listen. Be humble enough to *want to learn*, and honest enough to accept the truth. All things will then unfold, one insight to the next.

As for the company, this crucial DFL concept gives rise to our refining an entire "Strategic Guide" document that is now foundational to our operations at Lovesac. This Strategic Guide is like our Bill of Rights, our Constitution, our Bible.

It begins by stating our official higher purpose: *Inspire humankind to buy better, to buy less.*

It goes on to document our values, principles, mission, vision, philosophies, hedgehog concept, value proposition, and strategies. Second only to our amazing people, any success we have had, or will have, is owed to our strict adherence to this Strategic Guide.

By building strategies that are informed by principles and purpose it should never be surprising when you end up naturally "where the puck is going." We were chasing sustainability long before it was trendy to do so because we believed in it, on principle. We were succeeding with a small-footprint showroom concept supporting e-commerce as the primary platform long before it proved to be the dominant business strategy of this decade. In fact, I was told resoundingly that retail was "dead" or dying way back in 2001 as we opened our first store.

Well-documented and adhered-to values, principles, and purpose will *always* lead to the best results over time. They allow leadership to spend less time "managing." When everyone in the entire organization deeply understands these kinds of high-level concepts, they can utilize their *own* intelligence and judgment to make good decisions within their purview. Teams can move faster and stay on course naturally. *That* is the power of knowing your purpose and founder's philosophies.

I'm like a broken record now within the organization to ensure that each concept of our carefully crafted Strategic Guide is understood, internalized, and utilized. Every leader should play the role of "Chief Reminding Officer" for their team and make the effort to weave its concepts into every meeting, project, event, room name, program, policy, and award you can. *Use* each phrase often and wherever possible. Create a common language.

I have since utilized this same framework on a personal level to document my *own* life purpose, principles, and values. These guide my personal decisions similarly. I review key parts of both my personal and professional strategic guide daily, as part of my morning routine. To document these concepts I have cobbled together my own framework, taking bits and pieces from all of my favorite business authors along the way as I have never found an existing approach to be as comprehensive as necessary. I call it the 12 W's Framework, and for brevity's sake it will remain the topic of a future blog post, or another book yet to come.

Whatever framework you utilize, identify your purpose, mission, principles, and values as early in life as possible. I wish I had found mine sooner. That alone might have saved me a decade, I reckon. Perhaps *you* can. They may take some time to emerge, so be flexible. Some key components need to come organically through observation like Designed For Life did. But do not rest until you can nail them down and put them to use. Had I understood its value and started the search sooner, DFL would not have emerged in the earliest year of our business, but surely could have come a decade or so sooner than it did. Allow these concepts to evolve and sharpen over time and relentlessly hone them as *you* grow and evolve.

Expound on these ideas constantly to motivate your team and underpin all of your presentations. Nobody is truly inspired by "growth," or money, or goals to "dominate an industry" or whatever. People *are* motivated by true ideals and principles that matter. Purpose-led organizations and businesses can be a force for good—perhaps even the most impactful force for good on earth at this point. Businesses and business leaders, ironically, are now more trusted than government institutions or media. Identifying, documenting, and living up to a higher purpose, principles, and values takes effort, it takes grit. Seek them out and capture them in a well-trafficked Strategic Guide. Know it cold, and preach it relentlessly.

Know yourself and know your purpose.

THE BRINK

January 2017. The new "Lovesac, Designed For Life" business model is a smashing success in 2017. Instead of behaving like a merchant-led retailer generating season after season of time-bound collections, with all of those inefficiencies and unsustainable practices, we have abandoned the selling of rugs, lamps, accessories, and limited edition runs that cloaked our Designed For Life Sactionals under layers of undifferentiated products and traditional go-to-market tactics.

We're approaching seventy Lovesac locations now, all in the design language of our newly revised "Brand Bible." Successful TV and digital advertising has amplified our growth rate. Sales are accelerating faster than ever in our history. This is the result of doing *less* and doing best. (Guiding principle #3 in Lovesac's Strategic Guide.) We are finally approaching profitability and financial independence. But we are still not out of the woods.

One night at Parsons, I'm standing in front of my "Sustainable Business Models" class, walking these graduate students through my proprietary "12

W's Strategic Guide Framework," as I've done with prior classes. I'm sick to my stomach. I'm feeling like a total fraud. I'm wobbly. I present this framework as the most effective and holistic way to model any successful organization, and even your personal life.

Meanwhile, Lovesac is once again, tragically, on the verge of yet another financial meltdown. With growth at an all-time high and the structural demands of the business greater than ever, even with profitability and positive cash flows finally in sight, our primary private equity investor is winding down and has no further cash to invest. Hard stop. But we need a bit more runway. I've been wooing new investors, and I have a couple near the finish line, but until the contracts are signed and money is wired, nothing is ever certain.

I've lived this before and been let down many times. Professional investors are notorious for spending months in "due diligence," even as we're expected to operate without disruption. This requires hundreds of hours from my entire top management team, as the investors scrutinize every nitpicky aspect of the company and its financials, only to pull out at the last minute with cold feet citing some speculative excuse.

With four kids, no savings, no home equity (still renting), and zero safety net, I find it hard to stay focused on my students tonight. I can't help but feel nauseous at the irony that is *me*, teaching *them* about "my personal framework to build reliable business models" even as my own is teetering on collapse.

How can a now $70 million rapidly scaling business feel just as vulnerable as it did when we were at only $7 million in annual sales? This is maddening. But I keep my composure and try to remain as cool and jovial as ever in class. I take my time to patiently answer their eager questions afterward.

Then I walk to the subway feeling completely overwhelmed and helpless. I buy a giant cookie and a Diet Coke in the basement of Grand Central

Station to try and console myself on my 11:00 p.m. train ride back home to Connecticut. After all, I need to block it out and fall asleep fast so I can wake up again at 4:30 a.m., teach at the church, come home to hug my kids at breakfast, answer all of *their* eager questions, and walk into the office by 8:30 a.m. wearing a smile so as not to freak anyone *else* out.

This is the lot of the leader.

LESSON #22

STAY COOL AND BE KIND

Early in my career I was a real hothead. In fact, my design team once made me this T-shirt that parodied the international symbol for "combustible" volatile compounds, in the shape of my head's fiery silhouette, because of my infamously long, spiky hair. I wore it to be ironic.

At the time I thought the T-shirt was actually kind of cool. I'm just a brash entrepreneur like the best of them. I was flattered by my team's attention and creativity. After all, Steve Jobs's tyrannical behavior was apparently celebrated by everyone, and that became my private excuse. But, in reality, they were making fun of me. I was just a jerk.

Life is a contact sport. We are all just human beings of various personalities, backgrounds, and circumstances, ricocheting off each other every day. *Business* is a contact sport. Do it long enough, and there will be bruising. Some situations are complex, uncontrollable, or affected by a multiplicity of players, where one or more parties will be left experiencing loss, feeling slighted, or victimized. It's often, in part, due to their *own* actions or attitudes, but they lack the self-awareness to see it. Some situations are downright terrifying, with potential to cause financial destruction or reputational ruin. As already discussed, luck—good and bad—plays a role.

Whatever the situation, whoever the parties involved—learn to *always* stay cool and *always* be kind. It is a superpower. It is *always* the right path. It requires sincere self-awareness, constant vigilance, and tremendous restraint. It requires mental, spiritual, and even physical effort. It should be the *extremely* rare occasion (like years in between) where raising your voice in anger or frustration is necessary.

Along with that, eliminate harsh criticism (without commensurate praise and love), injuring sarcasm, *all* passive-aggressive comments, and every kind of vindictive behavior—even when it seems justified. This is a high bar to require of anyone. But the best leaders, those who build trustworthy teams, organizations, businesses, and lives, exemplify this ability.

Start as young as possible in the pursuit of candid self-awareness. Read the best books. Invest *now* in relentless personal development to achieve the mental, physical, and spiritual maturity necessary. Then forgive yourself and reset quickly anytime you (or others around you) fall short—because everybody does.

I am still far from perfect in this realm. In retrospect, I never needed to be a hothead. It wasn't just the brashness of youth—it was a mistake. I could have been even more effective as a leader had I learned this lesson earlier. But since then, I have experienced losing hundreds of millions in enterprise value in a single day. I have been confronted with terrifying macroeconomic scenarios that threaten to end our business in weeks, total personal financial loss, crushing debt, specious lawsuits, investigations, threats, death of loved ones, and many of the most stressful kinds of situations we all will face at some point on this merciless journey.

It is precisely in *those* hectic moments where we must be on high alert, and then make the controlled effort in those moments to just *stay cool and be kind.* Nothing makes me quietly prouder than when I'm able to do this. Be completely unrattled under great pressure, while still *present* for the millions of interactions in between as we bounce off of clerks, cashiers, agents, employees, and even our own families as we struggle. No amount of anxiety will change the outcome anyway. Worrying has no value.

Say thank you to everyone, for everything, all the time. Smile. Compartmentalize the stress. Work the problem out in your own mind or with trusted advisors in private, using calm voices regardless of how serious the issue. Identify *healthy* ways to blow off steam, distract yourself with intense activities, and relax in between. Shake off the roughest moments. Move past things and don't dwell. Never hold onto a grudge. Be like a goldfish—no short-term memory.

But especially in the presence of any other human who is forced by the happenstance of life to ricochet off *you* as you wade through the trials of this life ... always stay cool and be kind.

"SAY THANK YOU TO EVERYONE, FOR EVERYTHING, ALL THE TIME."

THE IPO

June 2018. After months of networking, hustling, and "shaking every tree" we somehow close on the necessary funding to keep the lights on and bridge us to a potential Initial Public Offering, or IPO. It's another Lovesac miracle at the eleventh hour. We've just completed our first $100 million sales year, and we're projecting real profitability for the first time in the year upcoming. In the context of the market, these kinds of business results are rare. To achieve two consecutive years averaging 40 percent growth, coupled with profitability at a time when it has become fashionable to burn cash in pursuit of growth, is special. Most growth companies are raising piles of capital on grandiose projected financials and spending it as fast as possible to buy customers, even at tremendous losses, in the name of "that's how Amazon did it." We are in rare air.

Lovesac is certainly on the small side of firms to be seeking an IPO, but a boutique investment bank called Roth is willing to represent us. We have better odds than most to drive real value for investors and employees over time because of our solid financial profile and proven growth trajectory. Following our strongest instincts again, however counterintuitive, Tiffany and I choose to relocate back to Utah. This will allow our four kids to grow up closer to nature, and nearer to their grandparents, cousins, and family through their most formative years.

My earliest partner still at the company, Dave Underwood, brings his family back to Utah as well. We spin up an "HQ2" in sunny St. George. It will be our hub for sustainable product design, inspired by the natural red-rock beauty of southern Utah, St. George is removed from the distractions of the business office in Connecticut.

The downside is that I'll need to spend even more time on planes again, working between our Utah and Connecticut offices, especially with one foot in New York City now, as we list on the stock exchange. Everything comes at a cost. I fly my parents out to stay at the New York City Midtown Marriott the night before our IPO. We have a quiet dinner at the rooftop restaurant. We reminisce about those early days—the money they loaned me for the forklift, my dad's ingenuity to fix our first wood-chipper shredder and later the Haybuster when we were up against it.

It's been twenty years since I founded the company in my mother's basement dance studio, and it's hard to believe what it has become. Like an oak tree through a crack in the concrete, it has grown into a $100 million enterprise about to be listed on NASDAQ. My parents really don't know what to make of it. Lovesac will be the first stock they've ever owned in their life. Mine too.

Our IPO is successful. It is a day to remember. We proudly bring the timeless ticker [Nasdaq: LOVE] to Wall Street, which itself required another small miracle to pull off. The ticker, LOVE, had been reserved and unavailable for years ... but thanks to some networking and relationship building I had done in the years leading up to this, we got it, through a favor, at the last minute before listing. What ticker could be more appropriate, though, for a company built on it?

I am, at least on paper, finally a multimillionaire overnight—although now I carry the weight of having to deliver on every promise for a thousand investors simultaneously. More importantly, people like Dave, Jack, Donna, Doreen, Justin, Charlie, Torin, Tyler, Kylie, Brian, Scott, Nikki, Anthony, Tom, Annie, Megan, Colin, Liz, Mark, Ellie, James, Ryan, Laura, Sarah, Chad, Stephen, Sip, Leona, Kevin, Kristi, Taylor, Zach, Mike, Sue, Pat, and the hundreds of other long-time #lovesacfamily

OUR IPO IS SUCCESSFUL. IT IS A DAY TO REMEMBER.

members who've earned ownership in the company can finally monetize their stock and take greater pride in what they've built.

Our *suppliers* have lent us millions at the most critical moments in the form of inventory when we couldn't always pay on time. After many years struggling together, they now have a more stable future indeed. And the *earth*, from which comes all the wood and metal and foam and fabric that we use to build our products, it has the promise of what will be the first Designed For Life business model taken to scale, sustainably paving the way for others to follow.

It was a great day—for all of us.

LESSON #23

WE CAN ALL WIN TOGETHER

Conscious Capitalism, by John Mackey and Raj Sisodia, is another one of the most influential books that has shaped my thinking over the years. It was introduced to me by Satori, the purpose-led investment firm that finally came through for us when we needed it most before the IPO. One of the main themes of the conscious philosophy is that organizations should consider the needs of *all* their stakeholders—not just financial returns for shareholders, which has been the dominant philosophy shaping capitalism since the 1970s.

Firms have many stakeholders to consider whether they realize it or not. Anyone or anything that is affected by your existence has a stake in your existence. So besides doing well by yourself and your investors or partners, consider the employees, the employees' families even, the customers, the suppliers, the community you operate in, and the environment, just to name a few. We try to do this at Lovesac.

I am often asked, as the leader of a very public business with thousands of employees that happens to have "Love" emblazoned over every doorway, across every T-shirt, and even in the headlines of our Wall Street financial reports: How do you create a good culture where people can thrive?

The possible answers are many, and tactics are endless. But my typical answer to this question harkens back to the very first Shawnism shared in this book: Just *do* things. *Try*. Make an effort, today. A new good idea is hatched at least once a week by someone in the organization. When you surround yourself with good, capable, caring, intelligent people, how can they *not* suggest some cool thing "we should do around here" to make it a better place to work, regularly?

The trick is to collect the best ideas, prioritize them, and develop teams and systems to methodically bring them to life in an organized way over time. Sadly, we're compelled by this modern world to spend more than half of our waking lives at work—it might as well not suck. Make it so.

Sustainability is a core concept here. Besides considering our earth as a stakeholder in the obvious way, the concept should be broadened. You see, if you cannot build your organization in a way that it can *sustain*, it cannot become a lasting force for good, it can do no further good for its people or its stakeholders including the environment.

Too many leaders these days overlook this aspect of sustainability and allow themselves to be driven by the powerful motives that push for wealth-extraction above all else—sometimes even as they wave the banner of "sustainable" products in the face of their customers! They have no credible path to profits or a truly sustainable business model and culture—only piles of money they've raised on hopes, relationships, and speculative financial projections. They enrich their founders and early investors at the peril of our capitalist system's credibility.

That is not *conscious* capitalism. That is not sustainability.

Lovesac's growth of late has not been slow, but it *has* been intentional and well-intended, like an oak tree. This is the model I believe in. The second-best time is *now*. This slower, more deliberate approach is not as popular with investors or impatient entrepreneurs—but I believe it is the better way, and will deliver more sustainable outcomes.

From compensation plans to philanthropy, from community involvement to sustainability ... besides the core premise of growing sales and profits over time, there are many aspects to an organization and many more constituents that have a stake in what we do than what is obvious.

Become aware of as many stakeholders as you can, consider them, plan for them, make the effort to build it for them steadily, over time, like an oak tree grows—and we can all win together.

"AS THEY SAY, THE BEST TIME TO PLANT AN OAK TREE IS TWENTY YEARS AGO. THE SECOND-BEST TIME IS *NOW*."

THE TECHNOLOGY

October 2021. We're sitting on a Sactionals couch in our audio manufacturing partner's offices watching George Miller's *Mad Max: Fury Road*. The pristine Dolby Digital acoustics are emanating, not from any visible speakers but directly from our very own Sactionals, hidden in plain sight.

In truth, from behind the couch it looks like something right out of the dystopian Mad Max franchise itself. Hundreds of wires and cables snake circuitously from underneath the Sactionals covers, consolidated into a harness, and fed into the back of a mixing board that would make any recording artist envious.

The key to making StealthTech by Lovesac work is to tune the speakers to compensate for loss of sound being emitted through upholstery. We've been noodling on the idea in our own product lab for years now, and we've patented it. We've already put a ton of energy and resources into it, and we know it is possible. Unique, but possible. Our partners here now know it is possible as well, and they're proud to share with us our first manufacturing sample.

My mind flashes back to when we first kicked off the project with them. I happen to be on a train heading into New York City for meetings. I listen quietly as our product team back in Stamford engages with this new manufacturing partner to describe what we're asking them to do. It takes about thirty minutes of back-and-forth until they realize we aren't asking for a surround sound system built *on* the couch—we need everything hidden *inside* of the couch, underneath all those layers.

"Well, that's just impossible," says Barry, a thirty-year veteran in acoustic design. "Everyone knows that speakers require acoustically transparent fabric, or perforated grilles."

My team protests, but the home audio manufacturing experts are adamant. They go many rounds. I can't abide listening to the debate anymore. This StealthTech strategy is everything, and I know it.

I take myself off mute and finally chime in, "Well, why won't you just try?"

Their engineering team sounds annoyed.

"Because it's just physics—it won't work."

I'm losing my cool now and speaking louder to make sure they understand how important this is to us. Holding my phone out in front of me like an object worthy of scolding.

"Why won't you just try? We can show you how we did it!"

"No, that's not possible—it's just science!"

I leave my seat and step into that weird transition space, between the doors of the adjoining train cars, so I can shout at the top of my lungs: "Will you please just tryyyyyyyyy?"

Silence on the other end. I'm embarrassed. I'm sure my product team back at the office, who have worked for months to arrange for this call, are mortified—certain the meeting is over. More silence.

Then, "Okay ... we'll see what we can do." They placate us. We send them our prototypes and notes.

When we finally arrive at their office this morning to experience the audio-enhanced Sactionals couch, much to our satisfaction, Barry (who was in the screaming match with me over the phone some time before) welcomes us, shakes my hand with a big smile, and says with a smirk, his head shaking, "You guys were right ... it's perfect."

LESSON # ? 4

PAIR STUBBORNNESS WITH CONFIDENT HUMILITY

know my behavior described in this chapter contradicts my advice to always keep things cool. Well, we all have our moments. But we must pick our battles carefully and sparingly. Again, listen to your gut. Learn to discern between the things that *really* matter to you, and every other whim or idea that happens to drift through your brilliant mind. Learn to spend enough time meditating on the biggest concepts, strategies, and ideas you have until you are sure about what they *really* represent. What is at their root? What is driving this hankering, really? *Why* are you intuitively passionate about it?

You may find that it is not the specific *idea* at all but the *outcome* of it that you're interested in. Enlist your most trusted partners to "chew on them" with you and to challenge you. This superpower, too, should be used economically, lest it become tiresome or downright intolerable to those you work with (like I am at times).

Pair your intractable stubbornness with the confident humility to be genuinely open-minded to all challenges. Welcome the debate—not as another grandstanding moment to demonstrate your intellect but as the necessary process to cultivate the best ideas. Consider each opposing view sincerely with intellectual honesty.

Through this kind of open and honest debate with yourself, your teams, or your opposition, one of three things will surely occur:

One, the idea will be refined through the process, you'll feel even more conviction for it, and a surety that your stubbornness is warranted. You're on the right track.

Two, the idea will be redirected and will lead you to an even better solution—one you would have never gotten to without the spark of that original instinct. This validates your "gut," and the new direction can be pursued with confidence. Presuming others participated, you'll demonstrate what confident humility is by deflecting all "the credit" to them. This will not only enroll them in the idea further, but it will build the necessary goodwill to drive change later.

Three, your idea or concept will be killed. It turns out to have been a terrible idea to begin with, or maybe just poorly timed. You can always put something on the back burner—if only for pragmatic considerations like timing, sequence, constraints, or available resources.

In any case, it is *your* choice. You can choose to force *anything* through if you're willing to pay the price and commit completely. Sometimes, that is exactly what needs to be done to bring something truly novel into this world or drive meaningful change.

But by pairing your dangerous capacity for stubbornness with the confident humility required to explore it completely first, listening to others without bias, and then going where the evidence leads you after much deliberation ... then you can apply your stubbornness more sparingly, correctly, and to great effect.

THE FUTURE

January 2023. There are not enough words to describe the whipsaw of emotions felt as a business leader and employer navigating through the COVID-19 era and out the other side. Just as we're getting real traction as a public company in 2019, we're forced to close *every* showroom immediately in early 2020. Our showrooms are driving 80 percent of our sales at the time. How can we afford to just close them all? Imminent financial doom feels unavoidable. Insolvency again—ahhhhhh! Stay cool.

Stop all investments in new products and our future, use every dollar to prepare for the worst. Freeze all hires. Eliminate all travel. Lay off all sales associates but hang on to our loyal leaders at each location—let them try to demonstrate and sell remotely by video from home.

Wait, no ...

Sales waver for a few terrifying weeks and then ... they don't. It swings the other way! With consumers now stuck at home buying everything online, they're contemplating the condition of their couch as well. This strange COVID-19 time frame will bring an unprecedented economic boom to the entire home category. Who knew? Who could have known? But now the supply chain is all twisted due to COVID-19 flare-ups in port cities and container shortages worldwide. Stop all investments again. Use every available dollar to support deeper inventory buys to mitigate against the uncertainty.

Now malls are reopening. We better staff up again quickly and build out new locations as fast as possible to catch the oncoming wave of revenge shopping. Record growth is now stacking up on top of record growth. With each of these jolting twists, projects are started, stopped, derailed, and redirected. Products and programs we've waited decades to bring to fruition finally—not happening again.

With a nudge from my wise partner Jack, it is in this crazy context that I invite Mary Fox, from our board of directors, to join management full-time as our new president and COO. Jack is moving toward retirement. Mary has been lead operator in many large organizations and has a unique passion for all things sustainable. Given her storied career, she could probably captain anything she likes. Mary is more than we can afford, but then, you can't afford *not* to hire the best, right? You never know until you ask.

Mary is in, and just in time to pull together a team-building offsite with our entire top team out in the Utah desert where we can plan the future as we emerge from the COVID-19 lockdown. The team is evolving and gaining traction.

So here is what will happen over the next decade or two: We will utilize our Designed For Life (DFL) framework to conjure up endless new inventions in the realm where home meets technology. Adherence to this framework will generate more useful, more durable, more adaptable, and more *sustainable* products than all other firms we compete with. We will pair those products with long-term-focused programs and services that can foster long-term relationships with customers, and we will operate our business in a more circular way in pursuit of true sustain-hyphen-ability.

We'll seek to foment a "buy it for life" movement among all consumers everywhere—as a backlash against planned obsolescence and unsustainable practices. Our loyal customers will come to love what we do and *how* we uniquely do it, and this is how we aim to achieve our stated mission to build "The most *beloved* brand in America" someday.

We'll *get* to employ thousands of great people and build an awesome culture with LOVE at its core. Our big-hairy-audacious goal (BHAG), "To see *all* products from all brands made Designed For Life someday, and delivered through Circular Operations," can only come to pass if we are so radically successful as a business, at Lovesac, that others are forced to emulate the way we do things because customers have come to demand it.

This is the path to *true* sustainability, and we intend to be a leader in this movement. It has taken us twenty-five years to figure all of this out, and now this is *us* talking big, but prepared to work small for another fifty if that's what it takes. We are focused on the future. We only think in decades, and we have top ambitions to change the way people think about buying ... everything.

MAINTAIN TOP AMBITION WITH INFINITE PATIENCE

You've now followed my story from Lovesacs to Sactionals to Stealth-Tech and beyond. We have so much further to go. Admittedly, it has taken way too long already. But like the oak tree that has grown up through concrete, I am stronger for it. The winding path I've taken has afforded me these valuable lessons and countless others along the way. I am wiser for it. I know who I am. I see what I can become. I've found purpose. I've found love. I've been humbled to become teachable yet stayed *just dumb enough* to believe I can do almost anything with the right team.

I'm all-in now, with one hand on the now and one on the next, still playing along the way, even as I fill every seam and crack with the grit to work small but dream big. I'll make my own luck, and we will all win together as one gigantic, loving, kind, and cool company of people, building something meant to last a lifetime and evolve forever as the world does.

I'm grateful for this twenty-five-year adventure as it has forced upon me the pragmatic perspective that I have today: Things usually take way longer, and they're way harder than we ever think they will. But I genuinely believe (as the cliché goes), if only I had known then what I know now, I could have shaved at least a decade off. Perhaps you can. I still find myself, all too often, advising my teammates and partners to "be patient."

As the words leave my lips, I hate how they taste. I am not a complacent person. "Be patient" is so easily confused for a lack of urgency or ambition. But I have come to learn it is the opposite. Exercising patience requires the grit we speak of. Truly great outcomes oblige us to maintain our top ambitions, *paired* with infinite patience—an unlikely duo.

One of my favorite things to do on vacation somewhere beachy is to swim in open water. There is something kind of thrilling and a bit unnerving about it. The waves, the seaweed, the creatures, the sounds, the depth, the cold, the shadows, and the imaginary sharks always lurking in chase. But after the initial twenty minutes or so of irregular breathing, treading water to look around too often, and mild anxiety triggering the desire to head back to my sunny lounge chair ... if I just push a *bit* further, I can get into the flow. The rhythm of the swim takes over. It becomes almost effortless. Almost fun. I can go for miles.

Critical to really covering some distance is the discipline to keep one's head down, focused on steady forward momentum and breathing in good form, without interruption, for extended periods of time. Block out the noise and the waves and the fleeting frights along the way. Stay calm. Equally critical, however, is the *occasional* pause to look up, assess the context, get your bearings by spotting a landmark far off in the direction you wish to go. Then adjust course, and swim again on that adjusted trajectory, for a *really long time* in that direction, without looking up to face distraction. This is what is required to really get somewhere, remain on course, and stay sane along the way.

Those with the ambition necessary to really make things happen in this world are certainly among us. But those with the ability to *maintain* top ambition, with an unflinching eye set on their most audacious goals, for as long as it takes, without ever giving up—across years and decades, tides, and setbacks ... *that* is the rare but necessary combination of passion and fortitude that can deliver truly remarkable outcomes.

So be patient. Go all-in, for as long as it takes. Twenty-five years and twenty-five more, without ever losing sight of your wildest goals. They will come to you. Even if you shoot for the stars but only land on the moon, you still will have made it to outer space. It will have been the adventure called your life. It will be satisfying. And it will be your fault.

Shawn D. Nelson is the founder and CEO of The Lovesac Company (NASDAQ: LOVE), which he founded in 1998 originally in Salt Lake City, Utah. He holds a BA from the University of Utah in Mandarin Chinese and a Master's in Strategic Design and Management from Parsons, The New School for Design, in New York City, where he later became an instructor in the graduate program. He is an avid reader, musician, outdoorsman, and outspoken ambassador for sustainability and the "Buy It For Life" movement focused on sustain-ability—things that can actually *sustain*. Shawn lives in St. George, Utah, with his wife, Tiffany, and their children: Lucky, Duke, Pepper, and Valentine. Want more? Scan the QR code below to listen to the *Let Me Save You 25 Years Podcast*, which expounds further upon the concepts in this book, or follow Shawn on social media @shawnoflovesac, and learn more.